trotman

An A-Z of
exam
survival

How to approach exams
with confidence

An A-Z of
exam
survival

How to approach exams
with confidence

Mario Di Clemente

An A–Z of Exam Survival
First edition published in 2002 by Trotman and Company Ltd
2 The Green, Richmond, Surrey TW9 1PL

Revised and updated reprint 2004

Editorial and Publishing Team

Author Mario Di Clemente
Editorial Mina Patria, Editorial Director; Rachel Lockhart, Commissioning
Editor; Anya Wilson, Managing Editor; Bianca Knights, Assistant Editor
Production Ken Ruskin, Head of Pre-press and Production; James Rudge,
Production Artworker
Sales and Marketing Deborah Jones, Head of Sales and Marketing
Advertising Tom Lee, Commercial Director
Managing Director Toby Trotman

British Library Cataloguing in Publication Data
A catalogue record for this book is available from the British Library.

ISBN 0 85660 975 7

Typeset by Mac Style Ltd, Scarborough, N. Yorkshire
Printed and bound in Great Britain by Bell & Bain Ltd, Glasgow, Scotland

Contents

Acknowledgements   vi

1. Surviving the exam experience   1
An introduction

2. The importance of being ready   9
Preparation – the key to exam survival

3. Figures and formulae   24
Revising Maths and science subjects

4. Classics and culture   37
Revising Arts subjects

5. Total recall   59
Memory aids and how to use them

6. All gain, no pain   70
Managing exam-related stress

7. The final countdown   84
Last-minute revision (and nerves)

8. The moment of truth   91
Surviving the exam itself

9. All about coursework   112
How to make the best of it

The end   117

Acknowledgements

Many thanks to everyone who contributed to the previous edition of this book – in particular Nick Higgins, and also to James Burnett, Ramesh Ramsahoye, Jane Hawkes, Imran Rahman, Sarah Tyler, Kate Smith, Alan Shaw, Robert Heggie, Richard Martin, Moyra Grant, John Cameron and Rosy Andrew. Thank you to everyone at Trotman for your help. Gratitude also goes to Tony Buzan, Irene Richards and everyone at Buzan Centres Ltd for allowing us to include Mind Map® information in Chapter 5. 'Mind Map' is a Registered Trademark of the Buzan Organisation used with enthusiastic permission.

Mario Di Clemente
June 2004

Chapter 1
Surviving the exam experience

An introduction

Exams. They are the bane of every student's life. From fresh-faced teenagers taking on the unfamiliarity of GCSEs, to battle-weary undergraduates cramming their way through finals, the story is the same. Too much work, not enough time. Distractions, expectations and writer's cramp. And pressure – always with the pressure. Whatever level you are studying at, the pressure you are under at exam time comes from all angles, swamping you with the kind of stress that could fell a horse.

Your parents want you to make them proud and they, in all innocence, will probably do their utmost to make you feel as if this is the most important moment of your life. Similarly your teachers and school are, to a certain extent, motivated by professional pride. Unlike your parents, your teachers' contact with you has only been in an academic context, so it is little wonder that they try to make you do well. After all, it is their job. And your friends are always there to remind you how well or badly they, and you, are doing. It is almost impossible to avoid feelings of rivalry and the desire to do better than your mates. Add this all up and it's clear that the pressure is intense.

Okay, so this is all rather cynical. Your parents, teachers and friends want you to do well more for yourself than for them. They care that you take your education seriously and so set yourself up for a long and happy life, characterised by prosperity and continual personal development – and working hard enough to achieve good exam results is a proven way of getting there.

However, what the cynical view does illustrate is that for a whole range of complicated reasons the events of a couple of hours at the end of two or more years of study reach a lot further than they perhaps warrant. The pressure applied to you, and millions of other students like you, for just a few short weeks in the summer is immense.

Put this out of your mind. Now.

What the pressure is or where it comes from is irrelevant. It is how you perform under this pressure that is important. The approach you take to your exams, the work you put in and how you handle the stress will determine your overall success. And this is what this book is all about: *surviving* the exam experience. Whoever you are, whatever you've done so far, wherever you're at, what are the things you can do to make the best of a difficult situation?

We can do this the easy way

Of course, while the final exams are the focal point of the academic year, it is not just 'the events of a couple of hours' that make the difference. Your exams are the culmination of a number of years of hard work and commitment and in theory should be no big deal. If you were to stick conscientiously to the principles of 'good revision', never deviating, never putting things off and never worrying, exams would be a piece of cake. From the very first day of your course to the very last exam you would work towards the single goal of achieving excellent results, and the journey would be a smooth one.

Indeed this is what the vast majority of exam and revision information and advice is based on: how to cruise through the exam experience. Every year countless books and newspaper supplements are produced with the aim of taking everyday students and turning them into exam-taking machines, perfect in every way.

Yeah, right!

While it is extremely important always to emphasise the right way of doing things (best practice), it is not always practical. Every student needs to be aware of what it takes to achieve perfection if they are to have any hope of doing so, but when was the last time that this actually happened? Seriously, do you know of anyone who goes about his or her revision in an ideal fashion? Did *you* the last time you took some exams? If you are due to take some more, are you in a position that makes it possible to follow best practice and thereby take the easy route? Or is time short – meaning you're in for a slightly rougher ride?

Let's be honest, the latter is most likely to be the truth. In which case, advice that focuses exclusively on the 'easy' way, while entirely necessary, automatically disregards most of the real world. It is as if it's this way or the highway – if you don't do all the right things at the right times, you haven't got a prayer come exam time. This is plainly not true. After all, people have been passing exams with flying colours for years; they can't *all* have been ideal students.

... Or the hard way

Most students don't, or simply can't, follow the ideal learning and revision programme as it is set out in most of the exam advice literature. They may well incorporate a number of the tips and techniques from the easy way in an effort to get the best out of themselves, but the fact remains that many, if not most, students will not be as ready for the start of their exams as they would like.

This is not necessarily a problem. For many people, a month or so – or even a few weeks – of good work is enough to ensure they fulfil their potential in the exam hall. It's more difficult to go about it in this way, and it brings with it the possibility of greater stress levels, but it is a perfectly acceptable route to take.

Of course some students find themselves in a relatively desperate situation, having done little or no revision, with only a matter of days to go until the big test. Ironically these are the people who probably need help and advice the most, only to find that they have been excluded for not having got their act together sooner. Even faced with such a predicament it is not too late to make a success of it. The needle on the stress-o-meter may well go off the scale, but many would agree that this is preferable to giving up.

The key point to remember is that there is always something you can do. It is never too late. As an examinee your challenge is to make the best of your own particular situation. Whether that means cruising through the easy way or battling to survive, progress is always possible.

Chasing the thick end of the wedge

Consider Figure 1.1, or what we like to call the Exam Survival Wedge.

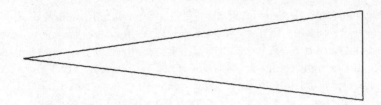

Figure 1.1 The Exam Survival Wedge

It looks simple (well, it *is* simple) but with a little imagination this innocent-looking doorstop can define the entire revision and exam experience. Honest.

The depth, or thickness, of the wedge represents your knowledge and understanding of a particular subject, or indeed all of your subjects combined. At the extreme right of the wedge – i.e. the thickest point – your knowledge and understanding is 100 per cent. You know your stuff inside out, it is second nature and you won't be troubled by anything a mere exam has to throw at you – you could even have set the exam yourself, you know that much.

On the other hand, the point farthest to the left – the thinnest part of the wedge – indicates absolutely zero knowledge and understanding. If you were to sit an exam from this position then that's all you would do, sit!

All the points between these two extremes equate with different degrees of knowledge and understanding and, therefore, different degrees of exam 'readiness'. Every person starts off in their own, exclusive position on the wedge and they all end up in a similarly unique position, depending on who they are, where they start, the quantity and quality of work they put in, the rate at which they learn and so on.

As an examinee committed to doing your very best in your exams, your aim is to get as far to the right of the wedge as your circumstances will allow, by hook or by crook. Every step you take in this direction could mean a few extra marks, which in turn could mean the difference between pass and fail, or a D and a C, or a B and an A. For the sake of example – and remembering that everyone has a different experience – this journey rightwards can be characterised in terms of three broad 'types' of student:

- the ideal student
- the average student
- the desperado.

The ideal student

A student following the 'easy way' – making perfect notes, doing every single piece of homework, revising and practising for the exam from the very first day of the course, etc. – will start at the extreme left of the wedge along with everyone else, but they will then make steady progress towards the right as the course goes on. When the exam arrives this progress will stop, probably a little short of absolute knowledge and understanding, but just about as far right as is possible given the confines of the course.

The average student

Starting from the same point, an average student will move relatively slowly at first as he or she attends lessons, does most of the homework, maybe a little background reading, etc., and then accelerate rapidly in the last few months as they get stuck into some pretty heavy revision. The chances are that this student won't quite reach as far right on the wedge as their ideal counterpart, but they could well finish in a strong position – especially given the right exam techniques and a bit of luck – one conducive to doing extremely well.

The desperado

This student will most likely find themselves perilously close to the left extreme of the wedge shortly before the exams begin. It should be obvious that a desperado's chances of reaching as far right as Miss Ideal and Mr Average are not great – they will most likely be starting their exam preparation from further left and probably won't be in a position to head rightwards at quite the same rate. However, they can still put into practice a

5

number of techniques and adopt some higher risk strategies that, with a little luck, will both edge them to the right and result in an exam performance that belies their final position on the wedge.

With all this in mind, our job is to explore ways of getting you further to the right of the Exam Survival Wedge **from any starting point**. And then we need to look at how to translate your finishing position into as successful an exam experience as possible.

Best practice vs last minute

The majority of this book will focus on best practice. Although this might seem strange given that we have already accepted it isn't always practical or possible to do everything that makes up best revision practice, there are a couple of reasons why it should have such a significant role:

- If we don't at least know the path to perfection then how are we ever going to get there?
- Knowing what you should ideally be doing will provide you with all the techniques and ideas you need to make the most of your own particular circumstances.

However, we will certainly not lose sight of those of you for whom best practice is simply not a realistic proposition. Therefore, wherever possible, we will also cover what you can do if you ever find yourself in last-minute induced dire straits – how you can apply successful revision and exam techniques to your own circumstances, how to make the most of what you've got, what to do in an emergency, how to cope with the increased stress and so on.

We will not judge you or ever dismiss your chances; we will just do all that we can to help you along that wedge, no matter where you start from or where you're going to finish. That said, on we go with the complete guide to surviving the exam experience.

A is for ...

Account for Explain why something is so.

Active revision Not just sitting and reading, but writing, testing, reviewing, etc.

Analyse Explain the main points in detail.

Assess Using evidence, judge validity.

B is for ...

Breaks Counteract boredom and stress by taking frequent short breaks during your revision.

Burn out Don't work too hard – a few heavy sessions is okay, but 6 months of 12 hours of revision a day is plain silly!

C is for ...

Calculate Find the answer using mathematical computation/reason.

Comment on Offer an opinion based on arguments and evidence.

Compare/Contrast Highlight similarities/differences between concepts, ideas, viewpoints, etc.

Criticise Using evidence, assess the relative truth/weight of particular theories.

Cramming Fitting as much revision into as short a time as possible. A high-risk and stressful, but often necessary, activity.

D is for ...

Define Give the precise meaning.

Describe Give a detailed account. In scientific subjects 'describe' often means include a diagram in your answer.

Diagrams Include as many (relevant!) diagrams as possible in your answers – diagrams demonstrate understanding and add to the clarity of your answers.

Discuss Explain a topic/question using different points of view, giving reasons, examples and evidence.

Distinguish between Point out differences.

Chapter 2
The importance of being ready

Preparation – the key to exam survival

At the risk of unduly alarming you, close your eyes and try and picture yourself on the morning of your first exam. What do you see? What kind of state are you in? Are you cool, calm and collected and set to take on the worst the examiners have to throw at you, or are you a trembling mess, complete with knees like jelly and the pulse rate from hell? Which would you prefer?

You would not be alone if you pictured yourself in the latter state while aspiring to the former. In the terminology of the previous chapter, you are afraid of being further to the left of the Exam Survival Wedge than you need to be. It makes sense, therefore, that the most confident and comfortable group of candidates come exam day will be the ideal students, followed by the John and Jill Q Averages and, lastly, those unfortunate desperadoes. And the single factor that separates these groups more than any other is how *prepared* they are.

Think of every journey you've ever had to make. From a quick 10 minutes down to the shops to a 15-hour flight to warmer climes, the one thing they all had in common was an element of planning. Even if it was just a simple phone call to confirm a meeting time and place, or a quick check to see if you had your keys, it is very unlikely that you would have embarked on a single journey without in some way preparing for it first. Without necessarily knowing it, you would have asked yourself some questions:

- Where are you now?
- Where are you going?
- How are you going to get there?
- What are you going to do when you get there?

Without thinking about such things you would probably spend aimless hours wandering round and round before ending up lost in a place you didn't recognise, without any money, or food, or means of getting back home.

This sums up the exam experience for a lot of students: a long journey, fraught with uncertainty, which never seems to make any sense and ultimately leaves you up a certain creek without a paddle! It should be easy to see that any kind of preparation or planning, no matter how small, will improve on this worst-case scenario. Not only will planning mean you better understand your subjects and exam questions, but it will also help you establish a more positive, confident mindset. And, usually, the more thought out and extensive the plan is, the better the end result.

Much as you might laugh at your dad for making sure you've packed for your holiday at least three days before you leave, or your mum for having a checklist of items you need to take with you, it *does* make sure things run more smoothly on the day. You don't take the risk that you'll miss your flight or leave your passport behind. You arrive knowing where to go and with the right kind of currency to get there. And, most importantly, you remove the stress associated with not knowing what your next move will be.

The trouble is that such planning, whether for a holiday or some exams, comes at a price – namely, the inconvenience of putting in some effort *today* in preparation for something that doesn't happen until *tomorrow*. The longer there is to go before your exams start, the less important they seem and the less inclined you are to do any work for them. There's nothing wrong with feeling like that – even the very best, straight-A students have trouble motivating themselves to start revising *two years* before exams start! What you need to do, however, is decide what your preference is for. Would you rather live for today and risk not being ready at exam time, or are you willing to trade off a little free time now for less stress later?

This decision will define your entire exam experience and as such should be the very first thing you do, regardless of how long you've got to go. Actually, do it *now*, even before you finish reading this book, hard as it must be to tear yourself away! And while doing it, always bear in mind what we have already established: that exam survival is a numbers game. Like the lottery, the more tickets you buy the more chances you have of winning. The more preparation you do, the better your chances of passing.

At the centre of exam preparation is your revision. However, good and effective preparation is about more than simply going over your notes a couple of times. So, before we tackle the ins and outs of revision, let's consider what you should do before getting stuck in with a vengeance.

Objectives and perspectives (1)

When it comes to exam survival it is vital that you know what you're doing, why you're doing it and what you can expect, before you start. Remember the questions you need to ask yourself before setting off on a journey:

- Where are you now?
- Where are you going?
- How are you going to get there?
- What are you going to do when you get there?

Let's take them one at a time ...

Where are you now?

You need to be acutely aware of your present situation – how long you've got to go, what the tools at your disposal are, your abilities and limitations, what subjects you are studying and so on – i.e. your starting position on the Exam Survival Wedge. Without knowing this sort of stuff you will find it very difficult, if not impossible, to establish how you will go about getting to where you are going with the minimum of fuss.

Where are you going?

You need to be equally aware of what your ultimate aims are – how well you *want* to do, how well you think you *can* do, the areas you will be tested on, the kinds of questions you will have to answer and so on. By comparing your targets (i.e. your final position on the wedge) with where you are now you can come up with a *realistic* way of bridging the gap ...

How are you going to get there?

Once you know the volume of work you need to do, the kind of work it needs to be and the amount of time you've got to do it in, you are able to draw up a plan of action, without the risk of taking on too much or too little. This should make the revision process a whole lot less painful.

What are you going to do when you get there?

You need to know what to expect in the exam and how you're going to go about tackling it if you are to revise the right areas and practise the proper techniques. (Chapter 8 has more about the exam itself.)

Your general objective should be for your brain to achieve optimal capacity just as your exams start – not maximum, but *optimal*. That means knowing all the *right* things and not necessarily *every*thing, a lot of which will be of no use to you anyway. It also acknowledges that the best you can do probably depends on a lot of factors outside your control (e.g. time, your course, etc.), meaning that your particular circumstances are accounted for in your plan.

When you think about the questions above – the first two in particular – you should always do so in terms of these factors. In other words, you need to build your bridge between where you are now and where you are going according to what's on your course and syllabus. This is because what exams essentially do is draw together all the strands of your study into a single question paper. In taking an exam you are aiming to convince the examiner that you have fully understood your syllabus topics. You should therefore ensure that you only ever revise material that is relevant to each subject and is likely to be tested on the big day.

So, one of the first things you need to do is look at your syllabuses (your teachers will have them) and all the past papers you can lay your hands on. Indeed this should be the key to defining your objectives. They will spell out exactly what material you need to know and the depth of knowledge and understanding required to achieve optimal capacity, and make sure you know just what it is you're dealing with. They will also provide you with some valuable short cuts if you're a desperado – if you only have time to revise four topics per subject they'd better be four that you're confident will turn up in the exam.

It is also a good idea to talk your aims and objectives through with your teachers, both before and during the revision process itself. They usually know what they're talking about so it's wise to put into practice any suggestions they make. Don't panic if this means making a few adjustments to any original plan you had. Even the best-laid preparations sometimes need to adapt to changing circumstances (for example, many students find that French vocabulary and mathematical equations take much longer to learn than they originally thought!).

And, of course, it is essential that you keep everything in perspective, or you run the risk of being so wildly off the mark with your preparations that no amount of teacher-aided tweaking will save you. Your objectives, aims, targets, whatever you want to call them, must, repeat *must*, be realistic. Don't be too ambitious and define where you are going as a point so far away from where you are now that building a bridge long enough to cover the gap is an impossible task. Similarly, you shouldn't sell yourself short by forming such an easy plan that you will never realise your potential. Remember: where are you now, where do you want to be and how can you get there? Furthermore, what's the *furthest* you can get? Always think 'optimal'. That is, the *best* you can do given your circumstances.

If your circumstances mean you have little or no time left to do your revision in, don't panic. In such a situation you might be tempted to abandon the whole objective-setting process as outlined here in favour of desperate and aimless cramming. Don't! Remember that even the shortest journey requires you to plan the necessary steps. If anything, the less time you have to go until the exam the more important it is to set realistic, achievable objectives. This might mean accepting that you won't necessarily do as well as you originally bargained for, but it's no use dwelling on what might have been. Focus on what you *can* do in the time you have, not what you could have done in what is now, let's face it, a parallel universe.

Okay, now that you (hopefully) have a framework of objectives within which to operate, you can finally get on with the job of actually working towards your exams.

> *An Examiner Speaks ...*
>
> *'It is immediately obvious to us when a candidate hasn't put in the time to be fully prepared for the exam. Try as they might to disguise the fact with waffle and flowery language, there's no pulling the wool over our eyes. In such cases it is very difficult for us to award the marks that we'd otherwise like to.*
>
> *'Of course it is just as obvious if someone has done his or her preparation. This makes for an altogether more pleasant marking experience!'*

Take note

Continuing with the journey theme (stop me if it's getting too tortured) your set of notes is the most important tool in your possession as you make your way towards your destination: the exam. Your notes are your car, if you will. A good quality set of notes taken throughout your course makes preparing for and surviving exams all the more easy.

Think about it: note taking is everyday work you're doing anyway (or at least you should be) and in the first instance requires no extra 'exam-specific' effort to put together. And there's no surprise more pleasant than finding when you come to revise that you have a collection of detailed, easy-to-follow notes, handouts and worksheets to help you.

Indeed you will most likely not be able to cope if you are a note-free zone. After all, you cannot possibly begin to remember everything that you have been taught without notes.

If you are unfortunate enough to have nothing in the way of your own notes, do not despair. There are many excellent revision guides on sale for all manner of subjects that contain concise sets of notes. Some are quite general whilst others are directed at particular examination boards. Ideally these should be viewed as being there to supplement your own notes, rather than as a substitute for them, but if you're ever faced with an emergency then it may be worth investing in some as a last resort.

You will, however, learn much more effectively from notes that you have taken yourself. This is because creating those notes required both conscious and subconscious activity from you. As such there is already a significant link between your notes and your brain. When you come to look over your notes later they will quite possibly remind you of the time that you made them – where you were, what the teacher was saying, what he or she was wearing, what was going on through the window, bits of background information that you didn't write down, questions that you or others asked, etc. – you will find that this makes the learning process both simpler and less tedious.

Tips for taking good notes

There is an art to making a useful set of notes. Although the notes that you take in lessons may at times be hurried and untidy, it is far too time-consuming to write them up neatly each evening. So think about the following points as you frantically try to get down everything Mr Goal or Miss Fortune has to say:

- **Try to keep the notes that you take in lessons as neat as possible**, avoiding too much doodling or too many messages to the person sitting next to you. This can be difficult, particularly if the lesson is proving dull, but it does make a difference when it comes to understanding them later.
- **Try to look through the notes at the end of each lesson or each day**, and if there are gaps, or words or definitions that you are unclear about, ask the teacher or one of your friends. It is unlikely that you will be able to keep this up for the whole of the course, but from time to time, particularly if it's a topic you're struggling with, it's worth doing.
- **File the notes in the appropriate place**, or you may never see them again, which would be a shame. Your original notes, containing everything you need to know or that is likely to come up in the exam, will help you to prepare revision notes when the time comes – i.e. condensed versions that are easier to revise from.
- **It is better to make revision notes throughout the course**, when you finish each topic, than to leave it until just before the exam. However, this is likely only to be an option for the most organised of students. Many of you will probably have no choice but to do this later rather than sooner.
- **It is a good idea to leave space on each page so that you can add things later**. For example, a later part of the course may well change your perspective in relation to a certain topic – the extra space will allow you to make a note of this.

- **It is easier to learn material that is presented in small pieces**. Don't try to cram too much on to a single page as you are much less likely to be able to revise from it effectively later on.
- **Use highlighter pens** to emphasise important words, dates, names or definitions, or underline them in a different colour. When you come back to your notes (which can be up to 18 months after you first made them) you will find such devices useful in bringing the key words and issues to your attention – these will form the basis of your revision notes.
- **Whenever you can, use diagrams, bullet points and summaries** to make the next stage – revision from these notes – easier and more interesting.

When you come to make your revision notes your aim should be to distil the essential information into a form that you can easily remember – if you have time once you've mastered the basics you can always add more detail. Have a look at the memory aids in Chapter 5 to get an idea of some of the techniques you can use to make a really useful set of revision notes.

It is often best to make your revision notes on small cards – several examples of which are included in Chapter 3 – or in a small notebook so that you can comfortably carry them around with you and they don't start to take over the world!

In revising from your notes, work through topics by trying to learn what you have done and then writing them out again without looking at the original. Don't cheat – you won't be able to in the exam. Then compare the version you've written out with the original. If you got something wrong do it again, and again, and again, until you can do it perfectly. Chapter 5 will tell you more.

To know is to understand

As essential as notes are to the exam and revision experience, you really need to be careful about how much you rely on them in themselves. Blindly taking notes and then reading them over and over again, paying little attention to what they actually mean, is pretty much a waste of time. It is vital that you *know* what they are saying, otherwise they are just words on a page and of no use to you. This is why it is better to have your *own* set of notes rather than someone else's – they're far easier to understand that way.

Exams are by nature cunning beasts, both a test of memory and of understanding. And you can only do *really* well in exams if you truly understand the material. If necessary, it is quite possible to survive for a while by simply learning the things that you don't understand off by heart, and relying on a bit of common sense and luck, but it won't work if you want to get the very best results. Remembering all the necessary facts will position you perhaps halfway along the Exam Survival Wedge, but understanding what they mean and where they fit into the broader context will move you considerably further along to the right.

The revision process itself is a great way of addressing both the memory and the understanding aspects of exam survival. You begin by learning and understanding a little, then you try and memorise it, then test yourself, then reflect on the gaps in your knowledge, from which you learn and understand a little bit more. You then repeat this circular process over and over again.

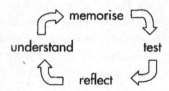

Figure 2.1 The circle of revision

As time goes by and the number of circuits increases the circle gets tighter and tighter and the process quicker and quicker. When the circle becomes so tight that it is just a single point you have perfect understanding and recall – the extreme right of the wedge.

The quality of your notes feeds into this 'circle of revision' and makes a big difference to how the process goes. Better notes will increase the rate at which the circle narrows by making it easier to understand, memorise and reflect. The better your notes, therefore, the better your understanding will be come exam time.

If, as you are making notes, you don't understand something as well as you think you should, ask your teachers for help (that is honestly what they're there for), or look it up at the library or on the Internet. If you don't understand something at the time you are taught it you certainly won't in a few months' time when the exams arrive and it's all just a distant memory anyway. It's best not to put things off – try to deal with problems when they arise and you will do better in the long run.

Revising fundamentals

And so to the revision itself – the 'how you're going to get there'. Opinions vary as to exactly when you should start. If you have done everything an ideal student would do – i.e. got into good study habits, compiled an excellent set of notes, organised yourself in terms of your objectives and so on – then a sensible time for serious revision to start would be about six weeks before the examination period.

Realistically, however, we know that you will probably need a little longer than that to get yourself sorted. Except that we also know that it is quite possible you won't have any choice in the matter and six weeks is all that you'll have! With this in mind the best advice we can give is probably that you start *now* because, whether you have two years to go or two weeks, there is always something you can be doing. Of course if you only have two weeks to go that something will be a little more intense and stressful than if you have the luxury of two years!

Regardless of when you actually start the heavy stuff of serious revision, you need to be properly set for it or else you risk wasting valuable time on inefficient study. You need to take a suitable approach and put yourself in an environment conducive to getting that 'circle of revision' as tight as possible, as quickly as possible. This is particularly important if you have left things a little late – remember, the less time you have the more you need to plan and the more efficient you have to be.

So, let's get back to basics and explore the form your revision should take ...

What is revision?

Revision can be a general term for the whole process of exam preparation, but *good* revision – what is that, what does that mean? Well, it is easier to start by identifying what it is *not*.

- Good revision is *not* a last-minute attempt to learn things that you were taught six months ago but didn't understand at the time.
- Good revision is *not* a desperate search for notes that you think you might have made several weeks ago.
- Good revision is *not* simply a process of learning lists of names, places, equations or dates.
- Good revision is *not* just a matter of reading through notes and textbooks.

Good, *effective*, revision – i.e. what you want to be aiming for – is the combined process of improving your knowledge of topics that you *know* will come up in your exams and converting it into a form that is readily accessible to you when you need it.

Everything we have been talking about in this chapter so far has been leading to this conclusion. Good revision:

- is ideal exam preparation;
- is organised by well-defined objectives;
- utilises good note-taking techniques;
- incorporates understanding, memorising, testing *and* reflecting.

Even if your knowledge is not that great and you have very little time left in which to revise, stick to these principles and you will do better than if you take a more random approach.

If you are not suitably organised, however, you will find it difficult to get yourself into a situation where effective revision is possible.

Where to revise

It's best to find somewhere quiet where you can concentrate. This might be a library, your bedroom or a quiet room at home. The bus on the way home, sitting in a coffee bar with a group of friends, watching *Match of the Day* or *EastEnders:* unless you are some kind of superhuman, these are all situations where effective revision *cannot* take place.

Once you've laid claim to your quiet place, keep everything as tidy as possible so that you know where it all is. Buy enough files and notebooks to hold your work comfortably and don't be tempted to put everything into one, heavy, 'mega-file'. It's quite a good idea to sort your work according to the topic headings on your syllabuses – that way you won't lose sight of your specific objectives.

You will work more efficiently if everything is organised – think in terms of making your mind reflect your notes; if everything is well organised and filed away for easy retrieval taking the exam will be so much easier. You may even be able to recall certain things according to where they belonged on your desk!

Before you settle down to work (in your neat, tidy and quiet place), make sure that you have everything you need – books, notes, pens and pencils, paper, a cup of coffee, etc. It's all too tempting to waste the first 15 minutes of your revision session by travelling backwards and forwards between drawers and shelves, gradually getting together everything that you need. Get it all out of the way before you start.

There is nothing wrong in having some quiet music playing while you work *if* it helps you to concentrate, but research has shown that music with a fast, repetitive beat unsurprisingly affects the learning process, making it harder to learn or to understand. So put your So Solid Crew and Slipknot away and think about perhaps discovering Mozart or some jazz!

Testing yourself

You should definitely avoid working with music on when you are testing yourself. After all, the point of exam practice like this is to try to re-create exam conditions – and when was the last time you took an exam with the dulcet tones of Robbie Williams ringing in your ears?

Testing yourself is the fine-tuning part of learning your notes. It not only makes revision more interesting, it also highlights your strengths and weaknesses. The whole point of this phase of your revision is to identify and work on the weaknesses rather than the strengths. Too often students spend hours working on the bits they enjoy (almost certainly the bits they *can* do), whilst ignoring the harder stuff.

A good method is to start each day with a test. This can be a previously attempted homework question or a mock examination question. The best source of material, however, is a past paper, of which you should have as many as possible. Before attempting the question think carefully about what information you will *not* need to include. Nothing frustrates an examiner more than reading a clear, interesting but irrelevant answer.

Test yourself under as close to timed conditions as possible and don't look anything up during the test – it's okay to get things wrong at this stage. Only once you have finished should you start to use your notes, textbooks or specimen answers. Work through the test and look up (and *learn*) the things that you got wrong, as defined previously in the 'circle of revision'. Don't waste time on the things that you got right, focus on the areas that need extra work.

You might be thinking that this sounds like an awful lot to take in, do and remember, much like the revision itself. And you'd be right. In order to cope you need one last bit of organisation, the last piece in the jigsaw – the revision timetable.

Perfect timing

Your revision timetable is probably the essential ingredient for exam survival and success. Its aim should be to ensure that each of your subjects is given the right amount of revision time without actually causing you physical pain! It is also one of the best and most commonly used ways of delaying actual revision proper – do not succumb to the temptation to spend hours redrafting and decorating what should be a pretty basic plan.

The first half hour of revision is often the most productive, so revision sessions should be short and should include gaps for topics that overrun. If at all possible you should avoid working late at night or in the early hours of the morning – it is not easy to perform effectively if you are tired. Remember that the point of revision is to train the brain to cope with exams, and they don't start at 4am! However, if you only have two days until the exam and three days' worth of work to do, it would be folly to sacrifice some precious knowledge in return for a little extra sleep.

If you have the time, try to leave as much free time as you can and factor in as many breaks as you can afford. Think about what else is likely to be going on at specific times of certain days and then attempt to build your timetable around that. For example, if you know that there are going to be distractions galore on a Saturday evening, there is no point in scheduling an hour of Maths problems for that time. Likewise, it is a waste to plan time off during a study period when none of your friends will be around.

AN A–Z OF EXAM SURVIVAL

You don't have to allocate the same amount of time to every subject. If one needs more work than another, give it more time. Don't spend an hour practising French vocabulary when you only need 40 minutes, just because you took an hour to cover trigonometry. Similarly, you don't have to do the same things for every subject. Just because a certain technique works for geography revision doesn't necessarily mean it'll work as well for English.

What we're trying to say is that it's horses for courses. Only you will know what your objectives are, what your strengths and weaknesses are, what your average week is like, what distracts you, what inspires you, what bores you, how much time you have left and so on and so forth. Think about all these things and then do your utmost to tailor your timetable accordingly. When you do, it might look something like what we show in Figure 2.2.

	Mon	Tue	Wed	Thu	Fri	Sat	Sun
9.00	School	School	School	School	School	Test-French	Test-Geography
11.00						French revision	Geography revision
1.00						Break	Break
2.00			Free Time			Test-History	Test-Science
4.00	Free time	Free time	Free time	Free time	Free time	History revision	Science revision
5.00	Filing/ preparation	Filing/ preparation	Filing/ preparation	Filing/ preparation	Filing/prep for the weekend	Geography revision	History revision
6.00	French	Science	Maths	Science	Maths	English	Overspill time for anything you didn't have time to finish during the week
7.30	Break	Break	Break	Break	Free time	Free time	Overspill time
8.30–9.30	Geography	English	History	French	Free time	Free time	Overspill time

Figure 2.2 Example of a GCSE revision timetable

That's it; you're now ready to get stuck in.

E is for ...

Evaluate Judge worth using supporting facts and arguments.

Examine Make a detailed investigation.

Examiner A nice person who wants you to do well!

Exercise Stress release activity par excellence.

Explore Investigate in a questioning manner.

F is for ...

Forgetting Despite the hype, it is impossible to forget completely something you know well. If you go blank, calmly work through the question/topic until you remember what it is you *know* you know.

G is for ...

Give an account Provide a detailed description.

Graphs Vital in answering questions in Physics, Economics, Mathematics and many other subjects.

Chapter 3
Figures and formulae

Revising Maths and science subjects

The good news if you are taking exams in any Maths and science subjects is that there is usually a definite answer to the question. This means that you have the benefit of a well-defined target to aim for and don't have to worry about discussing countless different arguments and opinions. If you know you've got the answer right then there's no need to worry about whether you've not mentioned the theories of an obscure Latvian academic or misinterpreted the question slightly. It also means that it should be more obvious which part of the syllabus each question is referring to, making it easier to locate the relevant knowledge in your brain.

However, the bad news is that knowing that there is a single, unambiguous answer can be extremely dispiriting if you don't know what it is. Indeed it can lead to giving up on the subject entirely, long before the exam comes around. After all, if you can never find the answer what's the point in wasting time trying?! Fair enough, but by taking this attitude you would actually be wasting time by *not* trying. The nature of these subjects is such that you can take them slowly and methodically, learn a little bit at a time, brick by brick. If and when you make a breakthrough you will find that the next one will come a lot quicker and more easily. So stick with it.

Maths and science subjects require that you know a large amount of factual information. In the exam you will not always be able simply to put facts down as your answers but they *will* form the foundations upon which all the questions you will be asked are built.

Most Maths and science exams require you to *apply* your knowledge of factual information – for example, a question on organic chemistry might ask you to identify an unknown compound by describing the ways that it reacts with other substances. Unless you have learned the way each type of organic compound on the syllabus reacts, and under what conditions, you will not be able to answer the question. Similarly, a trigonometry question in Pure Mathematics may ask you to do a calculation that you have never attempted before, and unless you know the trigonometric relationships – the Sine Rule, the Cosine Rule, etc. – you will not know where to start.

To prepare yourself effectively for the exams, therefore, you should base your revision for maths and science subjects around:

- the understanding and application of factual material;
- problem solving.

The rest of this chapter looks at the methods that can help to make you fully prepared for your examinations. The examples are taken from A-level or AS-level Biology, Chemistry, Physics and Mathematics topics, but the methods are exactly the same if you are studying other examinations, such as GCSE, IB, Scottish Highers or university examinations.

The natural sciences – Biology, Chemistry and Physics

Remember the 'circle of revision' from the last chapter? Let's simplify that slightly to create a three-stage process that defines a good way of going about Biology, Chemistry and Physics revision.

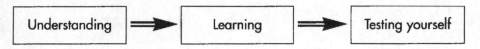

Figure 3.1 The three stages of science revision

Stage 1 – Understanding

It is difficult to revise what you do not understand, so your initial work should revolve around understanding the subject material. How do you go about increasing your understanding of difficult topics? It's easy, get help – from teachers, friends, textbooks, websites, revision guides, etc.

Most scientific theories and concepts are based on fairly simple ideas, and it is all too easy to get distracted by complications such as long words, intricate diagrams or equations. The important thing to remember is that the understanding has to come before you can start to revise. If you find a particular topic difficult, strip it back to its bare essentials, and build on these, brick by brick, until you can see the whole picture.

Stage 2 – Learning

So, assuming that you are reasonably clear on the things that you have studied (and that is a big assumption), what do you do once the exam starts to loom large? You need to get prepared. This means that stage two of your science revision should involve committing factual material to memory. As we saw above, this is particularly important because a large proportion of the questions that you will be asked in the exam will require recall of definitions, diagrams or what might be termed 'standard' explanations. For example, you won't be able to answer a question on photosynthesis unless you can remember the basic steps involved in the process. And while questions on photosynthesis will vary in what they ask, fundamentally they will *all* address the same basic processes.

A good way to begin is to simplify things as much as you can, and then add layers of detail each time you go over the topic. If you try to learn too much in one go you will probably only succeed in confusing yourself. See Example 3.1 for a model of layered learning.

Example 3.1 *Photosynthesis*

First, learn the basic processes:

a) *The light dependent stage - on the grana of chloropasts. Requires light, energy, water, chlorophyll, NAPD and ADP.*
b) *The light independent stage - in the stroma of the chloroplasts. Requires ATP, $NADPH_2$, RuBP and CO_2.*

FIGURES AND FORMULAE

Add some detail:

a) NADP = Nicotinamide Adenosine Dinucleotide Phosphate.
   The light dependent stage produces ATP, reduced NADP (NADPH$_2$) and oxygen.
b) RuBP = Ribulose Biphosphate.
   The light inependent stage produces ADP, NADP, RuBP, glucose and other organic molecules.

Then summarise the light dependent stage using a diagram:

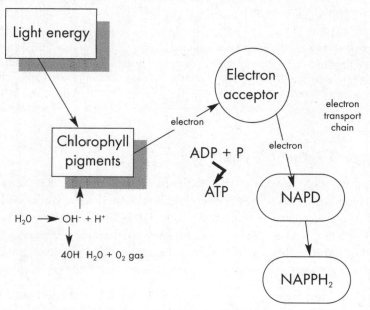

Finally produce an explanation for the light dependent stage as a series of bullet points:

● *Light energy (mainly red and blue wavelengths) is absorbed by the chlorophyll pigments and results in the release of high-energy electrons. This is called **photoactivation**.*
● *The electrons are …*

And so on.

Similarly, in Chemistry, you might be trying to revise electron configurations. The starting point should be simple – perhaps as shown in Example 3.2.

Example 3.2 *Electron configuration*

a) *The simplest model of an atom consists of a positive nucleus orbited by electrons.*
b) *Electrons exist in energy levels. The lowest energy levels are nearest to the nucleus.*
c) *To raise electrons to higher energy levels requires energy.*

You could then introduce the idea of orbitals:

a) *Orbitals are named (in order of increasing energy) 's', 'p', 'd', 'f', 'g'.* (You could think of a mnemonic [see Chapter 5] to help remember this. For example 'some **p**eople **d**ig **f**lower **g**ardens'.)
b) *Orbitals fill up in this order: 1s, 2s, 2p, 3s, 3p, 4s, 3d, 4p, 5s, 4d ...* (Give an example – Potassium: $1s^2\ 2s^2\ 2p^6\ 3s^2\ 3p^6\ 4s^1$ – to help you understand the concept.)

The next step would be to draw diagrams of the shapes of the orbitals, and perhaps a graph showing the trends in first ionisation energies across the periodic table and another showing the way the ionisation energy for a single atom changes for successive ionisations.

Stage 3 – Testing yourself

The third stage in science revision is to try and answer past paper questions from memory. This serves both to highlight which areas you need to work on and to allow you to practise what you will be doing in the exam itself. Your school will have been sent the examiners' answers to past papers – try to get hold of them so that you can mark your papers once you have done them and check whether your approach is a good one.

Try to do past paper questions under as close to exam conditions as you can – i.e. quietly, without looking anything up, and to a fixed time limit. Doing papers under such conditions should:

● help you to work effectively in an exam situation;
● teach you to cope when you face a difficult question;
● signpost types of questions that you find difficult;
● allow you to focus your revision on the areas that need it;
● add interest to your revision and ensure that you concentrate.

FIGURES AND FORMULAE

Do not be too concerned, however, if you repeatedly find that you run out of time. Whilst you don't want to get into the habit of taking twice as long over a question as you should, you will be surprised by how much quicker you work in the actual exam, fuelled as you are by a huge shot of adrenaline.

If you don't have long left to revise, and feel that writing out complete answers to past questions will take too much time away from more important revision, then you don't have to do it. However, you should still look through the papers carefully and judge whether you would be able to answer them if you had the time – i.e. come up with a summary 'answer' in your head. If you cannot do this then that must be one of the areas of the syllabus that needs more work.

Diagrams

All three natural science subjects are, by their nature, very diagrammatical. Answers to many exam questions require that you draw diagrams – structures, processes, pathways, experiments, etc. – and you will not gain full marks unless you do so accurately. Science questions that start with 'Describe' very often require a diagram in order to be answered fully.

Diagrams also help you to understand things, since most people can remember a picture more easily than the thousand words it paints (this is the basis of many of the memory techniques discussed in Chapter 5). For example, a Physics question might ask why a body falling through a liquid reaches terminal velocity. One answer might be:

There are three forces on the body: its weight, which remains constant and acts downwards; a force resisting the motion caused by friction as it moves through the liquid and that gets bigger the faster the body moves and acts upwards; and upthrust, which is equal to the weight of fluid displaced and also remains constant.

At the start of the motion the weight is bigger than the sum of the resistance force and the upthrust so it accelerates downwards. As its velocity increases so does the resistance force, so the resultant download force decreases. This means that the acceleration also decreases. Eventually the upthrust and the resistance force balance the weight so there is no resultant force on the body. It no longer accelerates and reaches terminal velocity.

As it's presented here this information is hard to learn because it is long and not particularly interesting. It is also important to remember that answers like this have to be structured very carefully if you are going to provide the examiner with clear evidence that you have fully understood the concept – miss out a single point and you will lose marks. And, of course, the examiner's marking scheme may actually allocate marks for a diagram.

Therefore another – better – way of learning the explanation (and of answering the question) would be as shown in Figure 3.2.

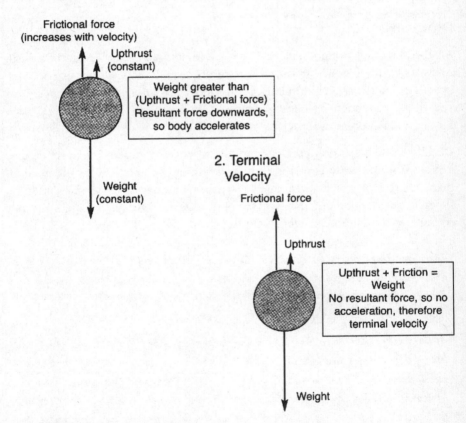

Figure 3.2 Example of a descriptive scientific diagram

Revision cards – Science

An excellent way to go about learning factual material is by putting the key things – diagrams, definitions, etc. – on revision cards (some people call them 'cue cards') so that you can carry them around with you and test yourself on a regular basis. An example of a revision card is shown in Figure 3.3.

Phenotypic variation due to the genotype

1. Interaction at one locus

Alleles (variation of a gene produced by gene mutation) occupy the same relative position or <u>locus</u> on homogenous chromosomes.

When the alleles inherited are different, the phenotype is determined by the dominant allele (e.g. a genotype of Bb for eye colour results in brown eyes as B for brown eyes is dominant over b for blue eyes).

2. Interaction between loci and epistasis

Some characteristics are controlled by two or more genes that are at different loci on chromosomes.

This interaction is called <u>epistasis.</u>

One gene controls whether or not another gene is expressed, i.e. it can inhibit another gene.

3. Linked genes

Linked genes are those that occur at different loci on the same chromosome.

They are normally inherited together as they cannot undergo independent assortment during meiosis.

This results in fewer types of gametes being produced and fewer than expected phenotypes in the offspring.

Figure 3.3 Example of a revision card for A-level Biology

Once you have made them, revision cards are simple to use:

- Pick a topic and try to write out all the things you need to learn from memory. Don't be tempted to cheat!
- If you get stuck, try to picture the card in your mind. Make it interesting to look at so that it's memorable.
- Try to remember where you were when you wrote out the card in the first place. This will help your recall.

When you have done this, compare it with the original and give yourself marks.

Memory aids

Try to use tricks and techniques to help you remember things. Chapter 5 is devoted to memory aids such as spider diagrams and Mind Maps® but it is worth mentioning here that *mnemonics* (see page 60) are a particularly good way of remembering scientific facts and formulae.

For instance, *the* classic example of a mnemonic helps you remember the order in which the colours appear in the visible part of the electromagnetic spectrum (red, orange, yellow, green, blue, indigo, violet): **Richard Of York Gave Battle In Vain.**

Mnemonics can also be simple rhymes or easily remembered phrases. For example, many students recall the way in which white light is dispersed and refracted when it passes through a prism by using the sentence: *'Blue bends most because red light is more rapid'*.

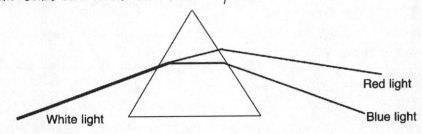

Light of a shorter wavelength (blue light) is deviated through a greater angle than longer wavelength light (red light) because it moves more slowly through glass, ie. 'Blue Bends more because Red is more Rapid.'

Red light

White light

Blue light

Figure 3.4 Using a mnemonic to aid recall of scientific facts

Mathematics

Maths is similar to Biology, Chemistry and Physics in a number of ways, but you will still hear many students complain:

'How can I revise for a Maths exam? There's nothing to learn.'

To a certain extent this is true, since the amount of factual material that needs to be learned is small compared to other subjects. However, there is still a great deal of stuff to learn - i.e. **methods**. The best way of doing this is through practice, which means answering as many questions as you possibly can.

As with science subjects, when tackling mathematical methods you need to start at a basic level and build in the more complicated material as you progress. For example, if you are revising Pure Mathematics at AS-level you will need to work on differentiation, perhaps as shown in Example 3.3.

Example 3.3 *Differentiation*

Start by learning the basic rule:

- *if* $y = x^n$ *then* $dy/dx = nx^{n-1}$

Then make sure that you can use it to differentiate, perhaps, 30 expressions. Begin with easy cases:

- $y = x^2$ $dy/dx = 2x^1 = 2x$

and progress to longer or more complicated expressions such as x^3, $1/x^3$ and so on.

You should know from your course that not all expressions can be differentiated using this rule alone. The next step therefore is to learn the rules for the following, more complex types of expressions:

- $y = kx^n$ (where k is a constant)
- $y = u +/- v$ (where u and v are functions of x)
- $y = e^x$
- $y = e^{kx}$
- $y = ln\ x$

and so on.

Again, work through as many examples as you can so you are well practised.

The beauty of studying Maths is that this is the sort of thing you do throughout your course. In effect, more so than for any other subject, you are revising from day one without having to put in any extra effort, which is nice. And it is a relatively easy way to revise as the exam approaches. You have little need to think about which theories go where, or how deep your knowledge of a particular area needs to be; all it is is practising question after question after question, noting where you went wrong, fixing it and then answering yet more questions.

And you usually get a formula sheet for the exam as well!

Revision cards – Maths

Revision cards are useful tools for Maths revision, but they should concentrate on *examples* of the methods to be used. They are more like recipe cards than revision cards, as they take you through the processes step by step.

If you like you could do them in the form of flow diagrams – for example, if you are studying mechanics as one of your AS-or A-level units you will cover the topic of projectile motion. Whatever the question, the basic method is to consider the motion of the projectile in two directions, the vertical and the horizontal, and you need to attach different conditions to both, as shown in Figure 3.5.

FIGURES AND FORMULAE

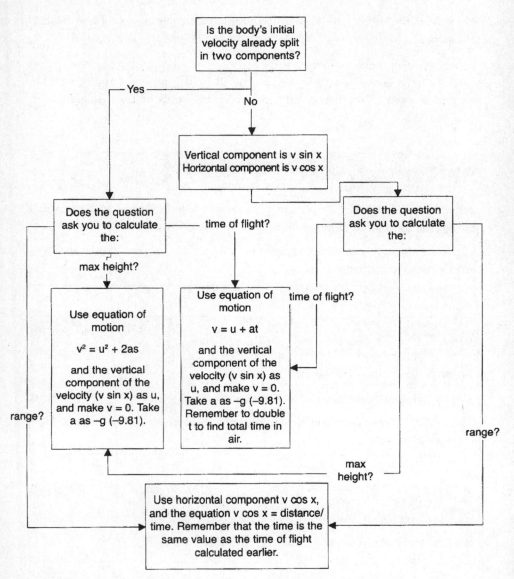

Figure 3.5 Example of an A-level Maths revision card

You should then illustrate the method with an example of a problem from a past paper.

If this approach appeals to you, use syllabuses or the course plans that your teachers have given you to make lists of all of the topics that need to be covered in each of the units, and produce recipe cards or flow diagrams for each of them.

H is for ...

Health One of the keys to remaining stress-free is to be fit and healthy. (And one of the keys to being fit and healthy is to remain stress-free!)

Heat Annoyingly, exams are usually in summer. Drink plenty of water to stop yourself overheating.

I is for ...

Identify Pick out key features.

Illustrate Clarify using examples, diagrams, etc.

Interpret Make explicit the meaning of something in the light of supporting theories and arguments.

J is for ...

Justify Show the reasoning behind conclusions/arguments.

Chapter 4
Classics and culture

Revising Arts subjects

Some of the revision advice offered in the preceding chapter will undoubtedly benefit you if you are taking Arts, Humanities and/or Social Science subjects – particularly if you are studying something that requires you to learn factual material (dates, case histories, etc.). In this chapter, however, the emphasis is on specific techniques for subjects that usually fall into the following categories:

- **Arts/Humanities**: e.g. English, History, Geography, Philosophy;
- **Social Sciences**: e.g. Economics, Politics, Psychology, Sociology;
- **Languages**: e.g. French, German, Italian, Spanish.

In what follows we will offer general revision advice for these types of subjects, tips on revising texts and advice on exam practice and technique.

Arts, Humanities and Social Sciences

Revision Notes

Good, clear, detailed revision notes are the key to exam success in Arts and Social Science subjects. If you have the time and inclination to do really well, a significant part of your preparation should involve writing and reading notes and revision cards. The form and focus of these notes will vary according to the subject you are revising (see subject-specific revision advice later in this chapter) as well as your own preferences, but, generally speaking, your notes for Arts subjects may cover any number of the following:

- terminology
- methodologies/critical approaches
- texts
- works of art
- themes
- concepts
- facts and dates.

For Social Sciences your notes will probably not be of the same style, as they have to record different types of information. For example, you may need to build up your knowledge of:

- models
- experiments
- research methods
- case studies
- ideologies
- theories
- systems.

Understanding different perspectives

Texts, works of art, experiments and even history can all be interpreted in different ways. At every level, showing a keen awareness of different perspectives can help you to obtain the higher grades because a good argument or discussion should take different views into account. Writing out brief summaries in your notes is a good way to separate alternative interpretations.

Language

All the Arts, Humanities and Social Sciences have their own specialist vocabularies, which you need to learn in order to be able to demonstrate your subject knowledge, analyse material effectively and sound impressive! You need to ensure that you know all the relevant:

- critical language and concepts
- terminology
- definitions.

Revising images

For subjects that involve the study of images, such as History of Art and Media/Film Studies, a good revision technique is to consult the works of art, videos, etc. in conjunction with learning from your notes. This builds up your visual memory, which will help you to recall information in the exam (e.g. it's easier to remember what the social and political background to a particular scene in a film is if you can actually picture that scene in your head). If you are doing timed work, practise using simple sketches and diagrams at appropriate points in your answers as this will help to clarify your points in the exam. See below for more on timed practice.

Revising texts

Themes

When revising a text, be it a play by Shakespeare or a philosophical work by Plato, you need to be aware of the major themes, characters, etc. You may already have notes under key headings but these can always be improved by working through texts again. You could construct spider diagrams, Mind Maps® (see Chapter 5) or flow charts to show the relationships between characters or events.

Annotating texts

You are sometimes allowed to take your texts into the exam with you. Always check whether or not this is the case as it will have a significant effect on how you revise. If you *are* allowed, any text brought into the examination must be the approved edition. Only brief annotations in the margin are permitted and they must only be on the pages that carry text. Your annotations can include:

- cross-references
- individual words or phrases
- highlighting
- underlining.

You are *not* allowed to use:

- plans
- notes
- inserted sheets or Post-it notes.

Different coloured highlighters can be used to cross-reference your text. This can help you to locate significant passages quickly and easily in the exam. For example, you might wish to use yellow to indicate parts of *Hamlet* that concern the theme of madness.

Quotes

Even when you are permitted to take a text into the exam with you it can be helpful to learn some key quotes, and what they mean, by heart. Learning quotations that sum up the theories of a psychologist or philosopher, or a particular aspect of a character in a play (Macbeth's 'overriding ambition' for example), can be a helpful way to build up your subject knowledge. Quotes can also help you to generate ideas in an exam as they are good starting points for further discussion – indeed you will find that they are often used as the basis of an exam question.

When you are revising it is often helpful to group quotations together under themed headings. Memorising them in this way also means that if a question comes up on any of the major themes you will be able to recall a series of appropriate quotes to support your argument.

Some students find it helpful to photocopy their quotes lists and display them in a prominent place at home, such as on the fridge, or even to put them on tape so that they can listen to them on a Walkman while they're on the move. Maybe this can work for you too.

Essay plans

For most Arts, Humanities and Social Science subjects you need to write essays in the exams (less so at GCSE or Scottish Standard level but certainly at A-level and beyond). Producing detailed essay plans for common question types should therefore be an important part of your revision. This is an excellent way of establishing what you do or don't know, and of practising the style of your answers.

Essay questions that you can plan answers to can be found in past papers or perhaps supplied by your teacher. Although you may already have produced plans for essays you wrote during your course, don't just file them away: they can be improved and modified by taking into account your teacher's comments. It is also the case that you will learn new things, think of new ideas and come up with more sophisticated and thorough answers to questions at the end of your course when your subject knowledge should be peaking.

Revising from your own work

One thing that many students do is file their work away as soon as their teacher has marked it. If you do this you might easily go on to repeat the same essential mistakes throughout your course without really knowing it. In order to improve your exam technique it is helpful (essential) to go through your past work and answers and consciously address any specific criticisms and/or comments.

Timed practice

If you have had plenty of exam practice at your school and can comfortably write a solid exam answer in the time allowed then you will need to do less timed work as part of your revision; but, if you have the time, it's always a good idea to do some. A good way to organise it is to sort through past papers to find questions on a topic you have been revising that day. That way you can test how much you have remembered whilst also giving yourself vital examination practice.

If you don't have the time to commit to this (either you have started your revision a little late or feel you will benefit more by spending the time learning the basic material), you can still look at some questions and plan how you would go about answering them. Even if you do this in your head it will tell you a lot about where you should be focusing your efforts.

Languages

Perhaps more than any other subject, revision for a modern foreign language is at its most effective when it is carried out on a regular basis throughout the year. Cramming in revision of specialist vocabulary or relevant quotations is certainly worthwhile, but to be a truly successful linguist you should try and make sure that the basic skills of listening, reading, speaking and writing are constantly practised from the start of the course onwards. Otherwise you will probably find that there is simply too much stuff to learn, even at the most basic level. Fortunately this doesn't necessarily mean much in the way of extra effort; just try and do all the work set in your lessons and prepare for all the tests that are set.

During the final six-week revision period it is best to keep to a structured programme of learning, memorising and practising which covers the following key areas:

- vocabulary
- grammar
- final preparation for the oral exam (usually held in early May)
- listening comprehension
- reading comprehension
- writing
- literary topics and/or texts (usually an alternative to coursework)
- non-literary topics (usually an alternative to coursework).

Subject-specific examples

The following examples of how to revise Arts, Humanities, Languages and Social Sciences cover a broad range of subjects and are likely to include at least some of the subjects you are preparing for. The subjects we cover are:

- English Literature
- History
- Law
- Modern Languages
- Politics
- Religious Studies/Philosophy
- Sociology.

English Literature

General revision advice

Good revision should take place at a well-organised desk or table, complete with any texts you have studied, the notes you have taken, and a pad and pen to hand. You should:

1. **Re-read all your texts** – adjusting the speed of your reading according to your familiarity with the material.
2. **Re-read all your notes** – could they be condensed? Remember that re-reading, re-thinking and re-writing notes are often the most helpful revision activities.
3. **In the course of your re-reading**, produce and learn quotation sheets, even – arguably – when you are preparing for a 'books in' module.
4. **In the case of each text**, think in terms of its themes or subject areas. These should correspond to the major essays you have already done. For example, in Shakespeare's *Othello*, the themes to consider might be racism, misogyny, soldierly values, the depiction of Venice and so on.

Revising texts

- Return to the essays you have written throughout your course. How could they be improved? Re-plan them in the light of your revision. If you haven't written any, think about giving some a try – at least do some plans – and asking your teacher to look at them.
- Plan out a number of past exam questions (your teacher will no doubt have made these available to you) and ask yourself what areas remain uncovered. Have those areas been dealt with in your own essays? If not, focus attention on them in the run-up to the exams.

Exam practice and timing

For one-hour essays you can usually allow 10 minutes for planning. Try to devote equal time to questions that carry equal marks.

Contexts

- Avoid irrelevant commentary and rambling and instead try to answer the question actually posed. Remember that the assessment objectives here relate to the precise analysis of the language of the passage.

Thematic questions

- Avoid narrative/re-telling the story; answer the question.
- The introduction should be reasonably full and sketch out the intentions of the essay. You may like to consider it a kind of essay plan in itself.
- Each paragraph should constitute a step in the argument and contain a central point, as well as maybe a quotation and an analysis thereof. Never begin with a quotation.

History

General revision advice

1. **Know the historical facts** – however strong your arguments, it is vital that you have the evidence to support them. These are the things that will pick you up some easy marks.
2. **Learn how to apply the information** – you must always focus on the question in front of you. Make sure any information you use is relevant and that it clearly supports your argument.
3. **Plan** – it is not easy to write an essay off the top of your head. During your revision, make structured plans for as many examples as you can.

Revising texts

Individual texts are not the focus of History. However, it is useful to learn key quotes in order to give your answers a little colour and win you extra credit. This subject is littered with memorable speeches that are overflowing with phrases that have entered the English language. Use quotes in your homework, in your tests and in the exam.

Exam practice and timing

The best exam practice is to attempt exam-style questions over and over again. All the topics that you are required to know for your History exam will be clearly defined in the syllabus. You should try to make sure that you are aware of all the kinds of questions that can possibly be asked and then, hopefully, how you would answer them. If you approach History revision in this fashion nothing in the exam should come as a surprise (after all, there are only so many different questions you can be asked about Hitler!).

Getting your timing right is a harder problem to conquer, but the better you know the detail and your argument the faster you will conceive an answer and write it down.

Law

General revision advice

1. Know your cases and statutes

One of the most important requirements for answering questions in Law exams is that you are able to back up the points you make with evidence, i.e. cases or statutes. It is not enough to state the law without citing the case or statute authority for the point as well.

You need to learn the name of the case, a brief description of the facts and the legal principle established. It is not necessary to learn the dates of cases, although it is always useful to know whether it is a recent or old case, whether Court of Appeal or House of Lords, and so on.

In problem questions you need to know the facts of the case in order to decide whether it applies to the situation in question. However, unless you are making a detailed comparison of the facts of the case and the facts of the problem question you should generally make only brief reference to the facts, if any.

2. Know your assessment objectives

Your Law exams are marked according to preset assessment objectives/ marking scheme. These are the rules of the game and it helps to know them as best you can. After all, it would be impossible to do well in a football match if you did not know that the idea is to 'stick the ball in the onion bag'. The rules for Law exams can be summarised as:

● knowledge and understanding
● analysis, evaluation and application
● communication and presentation.

3. Know your 'big picture'

You need to try and fathom the ways in which the different law topics in the syllabus relate to each other in order to give you a fuller understanding. This will not only help your revision enormously by providing more routes to the same information, but will also give you better fluency in essay writing. It is a good idea to produce summary sheets for each topic with bullet-point lists of the legal principles, cases and arguments it relates to.

4. Know your time allocations

A very common problem in exams is running out of time! It is thus very important that you consider exam time restrictions as early in your revision as possible. Try to get your essays down to about 3–4 sides in preparation for the exam, particularly if you are used to writing epics for your homework assignments. Try to develop an instinctive feel for the key issues and then focus on them. Do plenty of timed essays or quick plans in the run-up to the big day.

Revising texts

Whilst this is not a major part of Law exams and revision, it is often helpful (and impressive) to learn a few key quotes to put in your exam answers. These could include quotes from:

- Lord Denning (and judicial extracts generally)
- Professor Michael Zander.

Exam practice and timing

For 45-minute essays you can usually afford to allow something like 10 minutes for planning. Of course you might be a quick writer, or not have 45 minutes left, or perhaps you tend to need less time to plan ... Whatever, try and find something that works for you.

Essay questions – answer the question asked

Examiners will award very few marks if you just write everything you know about a topic with scant regard for the question. Adapt the raw material you have learned to the particular emphasis of the question.

Problem/data questions

1. **Read the question thoroughly** - never start writing until you are absolutely sure of what you have been asked to do. It is extremely annoying to get halfway through an essay and discover that half of what you have written is irrelevant or, at worst, that the question actually raises issues of which you have no knowledge at all.
2. **Answer the question asked** - pay close attention to the words printed immediately after the description of the situation. If asked to advise one of the parties, make sure you get the right one!
3. **Spot the relevant issues.**

Modern Languages

General revision advice

Vocabulary learning

This should be based on the general topic areas listed in the syllabus. Your language textbook may also contain helpful lists, and published vocabulary guides are particularly useful.

Grammar

Revise all the grammatical structures you have ever learned - it is usually the most basic errors that cost candidates the most marks in exams. Again, textbooks and published guides will be helpful here.

You should also go through a selection of your written work in the target language (say, 20 pieces) and make a written note of the type of grammatical errors you have made – prepositions, pronouns, past tenses, subjunctives and accents, to name but a few. A good way to do this is to divide a sheet of A4 paper into three columns. In the first column, copy out the incorrect word or phrase from the relevant piece of work; in the second write out the correct version and in the third column make a note of the topic or structure that you must ensure you revise in order to avoid repeating the error.

Listening

Use past papers for practice. Also, try listening to the cassette without attempting the exam paper – instead test your general listening comprehension skills, making a note of everything that you understand, and everything you don't. Borrow other cassettes – your teacher will almost certainly have a large stock of them. It doesn't matter if they are not entirely topical; it's all good listening practice. And if you know someone fluent in your target language then all the better – get them to talk to you as much as they can bear to!

Reading

Read as many target language articles or news reports as possible – they are easy to find in newspapers and magazines as well as on the Internet. Read them to help you develop your powers of spotting the general gist of a piece (a good way of assessing the extent of your vocabulary) or with more exam-based tasks in mind (e.g. summarising, report writing, translating).

Speaking

Prepare your topic(s) thoroughly. Consult target language material and ensure that you know your subject well. As well as rehearsing your presentation, try to anticipate questions that you think (or fear!) the examiner will ask. If your oral exam includes a role-play or interpreting task get a classmate, friend or relative to play the non-native speaker role and try to translate what they say into the target language.

Writing

With the help of past papers ensure that you practise the full range of writing tasks: summaries, creative writing, essays, task-based assignments, etc.

Non-literary topics

Read through and digest all your notes on each non-literary topic. Practise summarising them (without looking) in the target language. Compile revision card bullet points to help you remember the main points. Practise planning, or writing, specimen or past paper questions.

Revising texts

As early as possible in the revision period you should re-read each of your literary texts, if you have studied any. It is essential to be familiar with the story, particularly if you are unable to consult the text in the examination. Make sure you have notes, ideally in the target language, that cover each of the following key areas:

- **Plot**: a bullet-point summary.
- **Characters**: major and minor, their characteristics, role, relationships with each other.
- **Themes**: e.g. life, death, honour, fate, religion.
- **Background issues**: e.g. social, cultural, political, historical.
- **Style**: the main techniques used by the author. Consider narrative stance, language, vocabulary, realism, symbolism, etc.
- **Structure**: how is the story or play divided up? Is its structure effective? How? Why?
- **Useful quotations**: a list of around 20 per text is probably enough. It is unlikely that you will be able to learn them all, so try to learn some that

have more than one use (e.g. a phrase that highlights an aspect of a main character's personality as well as helping to stress the importance of a major theme).

- **Vocabulary**: produce a list of words or phrases that have more use in literature essays than anywhere else (e.g. imagery, stage, background issues). At least one exam board has published such a list: it would be well worth checking with your teacher.

Exam practice and timing

Practise planning and writing as many exam-type essays as you can. Be sure to stick as closely to the required time as possible when writing practice essays. The more you do the better your timing will be.

Listening and reading

Be guided by the length of each text. You should normally devote more time to the longer texts. This means disciplining yourself to move on to the next question at a sensible time. The more practice you get the easier it will be in the exam to know exactly how much time you can afford to spend on a certain section.

Writing

No matter how long you are allowed for a particular question, try to include 5–10 minutes planning time and at least 5 minutes at the end to re-read (and correct) what you have written. Exam invigilators frequently comment on how early modern languages students seem to finish essay-based papers, so do make sure that you use all the available time constructively.

Speaking

If you are due to give one, practise your topic presentation as much as possible so that you will get your timing absolutely right on the day of the oral exam.

Bear in mind, however, that a presentation should not sound like a rehearsed speech even though you may think that this is precisely what it is! With the confidence that comes from frequent practice you should be able to make your presentation sound very natural.

Always practise your accent by speaking aloud. It may sound a bit silly to you but it will serve you well in the exam.

Politics

General revision advice

1. **Know your key terms and concepts**. It is very important to make sure that you know the main concepts and can define them in a clear manner. Terms and concepts such as conventions, justice, democracy, power, authority, consent and legitimacy are all a vital part of the 'language' of political discourse.
2. **Keep a current affairs 'diary'** in which you record key facts, arguments and opinions. Link them to topic headings such as Parliament, PM, Cabinet, EU, judiciary, etc.
3. **Write lists of points/characteristics** that you can learn and test yourself with.
4. **Create 'model' answers** for questions that often crop up, or ones that are of vital importance.

Revising texts

Although you won't have to revise specific texts as such, it is very helpful to learn some key quotations that you can use to illustrate your arguments. These could come from politicians, commentators or philosophers. For example:

● *'As Prime Minister I could not waste more time having internal arguments'*
Mrs Thatcher

- *'The British Constitution is whatever happens to happen'* Peter Hennessey
- *'All science would be superfluous if the appearance of things coincided with their essence'* Marx

Exam practice and timing

Timing is of the utmost importance. There is no point spending the same amount of time on a 5-mark question as on a 20-mark question. For 20-minute questions there really is no time to plan, while for 45-minute essays you can allow 5 or 10 minutes for planning. There is no need to use lengthy sentences in your plans – key points, concepts, terms, etc. will suffice. Use your plan to impose a structure on the question – e.g. for and against.

Key tips:

- Briefly address the core theme in your introduction.
- Your argument should include a range of different points that address the question from all viewpoints.
- Stick to one point per paragraph.
- Keep looking at and answering the question.
- Use appropriate examples to illustrate your points.

Religious Studies (including Theology, Philosophy and Ethics)

General revision advice

Be aware of the following areas and how the material you have studied relates to them:

1. **Key concepts** within the chosen areas of study and how they are expressed in texts, writings, and practices;
2. **The contributions of significant people**, traditions and movements;
3. **Religious language and terminology**;

4. **Major issues** and questions arising from these;
5. **The relationships** between the areas of study and other specified topics in the study of religion and ethics.

Develop the following skills:

- recalling, selecting and using knowledge;
- identifying, investigating and analysing questions and issues arising from them;
- using appropriate and correct language and terminology;
- interpreting and evaluating relevant concepts;
- communicating, using reasoned argument supported by evidence;
- making connections between areas of study and other topics in religion and ethics.

Revising texts

You are unlikely to be able to take texts into the exam room with you, so you need to make an effort to get to grips with them beforehand. Bear the following points in mind:

- The examiner knows you haven't got the text in front of you, so you will be credited all the more for accurate and relevant use of textual material.
- You don't have to get every word of quotations correct – if in doubt, paraphrase and leave out quotation marks.
- Don't worry about chapter and verse references unless you are sure that you have them correct – leave them out otherwise.
- Focus on what's really important. For each chapter or theme you are unlikely to remember more than two or three key quotations, so choose them early on in the proceedings and memorise them.
- Once you've selected your key quotations, write them on index cards in bold coloured lettering, and review them regularly.

Exam practice and timing

The presence of certain trigger words in questions enables you to identify the particular skills you need to use. Some words invite you to demonstrate your knowledge and understanding, whilst others suggest that you evaluate that knowledge.

Knowledge/understanding trigger words

- describe
- examine
- identify
- outline
- select
- what
- how
- illustrate
- for what reasons
- give an account of
- in what ways
- analyse
- clarify
- compare and contrast
- differentiate
- distinguish between
- define
- explain.

Evaluation trigger words

- comment on
- consider
- how far
- to what extent
- why
- assess
- discuss
- consider critically
- criticise
- evaluate
- interpret
- justify.

You need to be particularly aware of the difference between 'giving an account of' and 'considering critically'. To give an account you draw on your knowledge, which you may then be required to evaluate through 'considering critically.' Considering critically, or assessing, or commenting on, involves drawing conclusions about the significance and value of what you have learned.

There are certain phrases that you may find useful to do this: 'This is important because'; 'The most significant is ... because'; 'However ...'; 'On the other hand ...'; 'It is likely that ... because;' 'Therefore ...'; 'Nevertheless ...'; 'The implications of this are ...'.

As you work keep asking yourself 'Why is this relevant to my answer?' and 'What are the implications of this view/issue?' Don't go on to automatic pilot, otherwise you will simply narrate facts or, worse, tell a story!

Sociology

General revision advice

1. **Familiarise yourself with key sociological concepts** – you also need to use the language that sociologists use, e.g. 'reliability' rather than 'accuracy'.
2. **Know your theory** – make sure that you are up to speed with the basic principles of key sociological theories, e.g. Marxism, functionalism, interactionism, etc.
3. **Learn key studies** – at more advanced levels you need to demonstrate that you are familiar with a range of key sociological studies, e.g. Durkheim's studies of suicide.
4. **Develop your skills** – knowledge of the content, whilst important, is not enough. You need to develop your skills of *application* and *evaluation*.

Revising texts

If you are learning about some key studies you obviously need to memorise the author and date of the study. This will help you position it in sociological debates. Also try to learn:

- the methodology used
- the main aims and findings
- the key criticisms.

Exam practice and timing

The best exam practice you can do is to look at as many past papers as possible. This will help you anticipate the kind of questions you are likely to encounter.

CLASSICS AND CULTURE

Key tips for answering questions:

- Take a little time to interpret the question correctly. Don't rush in without thinking.
- Don't spend too much time on questions worth relatively few marks. Distribute your time according to the number of marks available.
- Remember that good answers include the following ingredients:
  - a range of points
  - liberal use of key concepts
  - reference to sociological studies
  - reference to sociological theories
  - use of items (if asked for)
  - proper balanced evaluation
  - a conclusion.

K is for ...

Keeping perspective Exams are *not* the work of the devil – failure will *not* herald the apocalypse!

L is for ...

Location Try to visualise where you were and what else was going on when you revised a particular topic. This can sometimes help to jog your memory.

Luck Rely on it or make your own. The choice is yours.

M is for ...

Marking scheme This will mirror the syllabus. Tailor your answers to match.

Memory Limitless. It is never 'full'.

Mind Map® Method of note taking, improving understanding and memorising that uses words, pictures and colours.

Mnemonic An aid to memory.

Mock exams Use them as an excuse to do the right things.

Multiple choice Actually gives you the answer in the question – result!

Chapter 5
Total recall

Memory aids and how to use them

Every human being is capable of remembering more than enough information to see them through a bunch of exams. Unfortunately we tend to make use of only a tiny part of that potential capacity - which is an awful waste when you think about it. One way of unlocking the rest of our minds is to use memory aids - techniques and tricks that train you to think and remember in a certain way, making learning both easier and more effective.

There are a number of different kinds of memory aid knocking around but they are all based on more or less the same premise - adding extra dimensions to your revision. In other words, rather than simply reading through a stack of notes trying to remember abstract information - a narrow process that utilises only one part of the brain - memory aids are designed to make you take a different approach, thinking and working in different ways that ultimately allow you to learn more.

One academic argued that we remember:

- 20 per cent of what we read
- 30 per cent of what we hear
- 40 per cent of what we see
- 50 per cent of what we say
- 60 per cent of what we do
- 90 per cent of what we read, hear, see, say *and* do.

(Flanagan, K. 1997, *Maximum Points, Minimum Panic: the essential guide to surviving exams*, 2nd edition, Dublin: Marino)

If we accept this view of how our mind works then it becomes clear that, by using memory aids to engage more of our senses and help us think in different ways, we should end up learning and remembering more.

Revision cards

Not so much a memory aid as a revision technique, revision cards are a simple but effective way of learning your stuff.

The general idea is to boil down your notes into key points and words so that entire topics can fit on portable and easy-to-use cards. Once you have a set of these cards you can have them conveniently located for frequent, rapid revisions.

For example, you could put them in a card box on your desk – it keeps your space tidy and they are immediately to hand. Or perhaps you could place them strategically around the house, maybe stuck to the wall, so you can turn to them at any time, whatever else you're doing. Alternatively, you might prefer just to carry them around in your pocket so that you can take them out and revise at any time, wherever you are.

Whatever, it is their versatility that makes revision cards such a useful tool. They give you the opportunity to look at them first thing in the morning, last thing at night, on the bus on the way to meet a friend, in the bath, between exams, indeed any time and place you have a spare five minutes or so. This allows you to up the frequency of your reviews and increase the number of circuits around the 'circle of revision' (see page 17).

The style of your revision cards is totally up to you – what you choose depends on what works. You might like the conventional linear note form of the examples in Chapter 3 of this book, or perhaps you'd prefer to use some of the techniques in this chapter – it doesn't matter. Their key feature, however, is ease of use, so your only restriction is that they are small and portable – there's little point in having a set of A3 revision cards you need a wheelbarrow to carry around!

Mnemonics

Mnemonics are little devices that can help you to recall factual information that is either useful in itself or as a route into broader themes, arguments and ideas.

TOTAL RECALL

It can be extremely difficult to remember long lists of abstract phrases and words because that is not how our brains work. So-called 'Memory Men and Women' who we occasionally see on TV use 'stories' to help remember vast amounts of information – e.g. the order of playing cards in a pack. These stories employ familiar and easy to remember people, places, sensations, etc., to get the whole brain working for them, increasing their capacity for recall. By associating pockets of information with certain elements of the story large amounts of seeming gobbledegook can be committed to memory and stored there for retrieval later.

Mnemonics are like these stories: they take something that is difficult to remember in itself and associate it with something else that is much more likely to spring to mind. As with revision cards and most things about revision and memorising, exactly what form a mnemonic takes depends on what works for you, as well as on the information you want to remember. Usually, however, they are a short sentence, a rhyme or an acronym (a word made up of the initial letters of words in a specific phrase).

For example, the classic mnemonic is the one that helps you remember the colours of the rainbow/spectrum and the order in which they appear: 'Richard Of York Gave Battle In Vain' is easier to remember than 'Red, Orange, Yellow, Green, Blue, Indigo, Violet 'because it makes more sense to our brains. Of course it's no use learning the mnemonic by heart if you don't actually know the information to which it relates (ie the colours) but once you do it can be an extremely powerful tool.

Other examples of mnemonics are:

- F.O.I.L. – a simple way of remembering the order in which to multiply the terms in a pair of brackets: First, Outside, Inside, Last.

  Therefore $(x+4)(x-2)$ becomes:

  → x^2 (first)
  → $-2x$ (outside)
  → $+4x$ (inside)
  → -8 (last)
  $= x^2 - 2x + 4x - 8 = \underline{x^2 + 2x - 8}$.

- P.A.N.I.C. – helps you remember the respective charges of electrodes: Positive Anode Negative Is Cathode.

There is the risk in using this particular mnemonic that you confuse electrodes and ions, for which the charges are the other way round - i.e. anions are negative and cations are positive. A simple way of getting round this problem is to introduce another mnemonic: 'Possy Cats' (like pussy cats) to remind you that cations are positively charged.

This is an illustration of how you can combine mnemonics and memory techniques to build a bigger picture. It also shows how they can act as a trigger for remembering related information not covered by the mnemonic(s). Once you have recalled the respective charges of the various electrodes and ions, it is a relatively simple step to remember all about the process of electrolysis (assuming that you know about it in the first place, of course).

Your teachers are bound to have the odd mnemonic that they've picked up over the years, and will be happy to pass them on to you, but you can just as easily make some up for yourself. Be careful though not to overdose on mnemonics. It is easy to overemphasise the importance of retaining factual information and so hinder your actual understanding of the subject.

Spider diagrams

Spider diagrams are an excellent way of organising and presenting your notes and any additional information in such a way as to make its digestion quick and easy. And the quicker and more effectively you can take everything in, the more revisions you can fit in and the better will be your memory of them. As an added bonus you will also find that spider diagrams are far more interesting to work with than lines and lines and pages and pages of dull notes.

Spider diagrams utilise words, phrases, lines, arrows and pictures to structure and prioritise ideas and information, and illustrate the relationships between them. Building them exercises more parts of your brain and allows you to think more naturally than if you force yourself to think purely in linear terms.

They look pretty too!

Principles of spiders

Before we get into the process of actually creating a spider diagram there are a few general points that you should bear in mind:

- **Do it your way** – regardless of the example we show here or any that you see elsewhere the best way of building a spider diagram is *your* way. Develop your own style and visual code – it will be easier to work with than trying to conform to someone else's.
- **Use pictures** – they will arouse parts of your brain that don't usually take part in revision. Pictures, colours and exaggerated shapes are a very powerful aid to memory – they paint a thousand words, remember.
- **Use your thought process** – the way you think should determine the ordering and appearance of your spider diagrams. Putting your mind on paper, with all its peculiarities, makes it all much easier to remember – it doesn't matter if no one else can understand it.
- **Limit the number of words** – use key words (and phrases, perhaps even mnemonics) that will trigger related knowledge in your brain. Again, it doesn't matter if it's pure gobbledegook to everyone else, as long as you know what it means, that's fine.
- **Use hierarchies** – by prioritising your key words and information you learn the most important things first and best, which will then lead on to the next level of information and so on. You can use colour, upper/lower case, underlining – anything to indicate relative importance.
- **Use the positioning on the page** – just as it can help you remember a topic by thinking about where you were when you revised it, picturing where the information sat on the page can make it easier to remember what it said.
- **Build your diagrams around past questions** – this will serve to focus your revision on what is relevant, as well as allowing you to practise answering common questions.
- **Don't be limited by what you have been taught** – try to extend your understanding of each topic by using your spider diagrams, adding anything you have picked up from background reading. Leave space so that new ideas and understanding can be added easily.

Building a spider diagram

As suggested by the penultimate point above, start with a common exam question that you expect to have to answer. Alternatively you can take a topic from your syllabus – these are much the same things.

Then gather all your relevant notes from your course and any other information you have picked up along the way so that you actually have something to put in your diagram.

Think about all that material in terms of hierarchies, key words, pictures, colours, etc., and start to develop a way of presenting that thought process on paper.

Maybe try a quick rough sketch of how your spider diagram might look. If you are happy that it makes sense to you and covers all the required information, draw a finished version.

Figure 5.1 is a simple spider diagram that we put together to cover part of the GCSE Chemistry syllabus – namely, the types of radioactive decay.

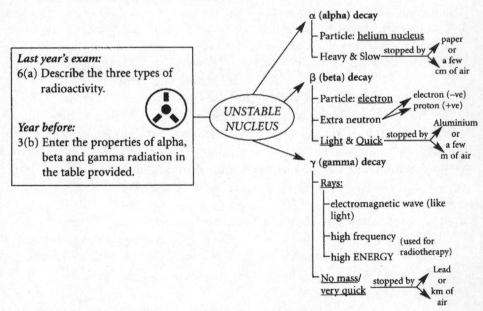

Figure 5.1 Example of a spider diagram (GCSE Chemistry)

This probably gives you a better idea of why they're called 'spider diagrams'! Notice how the hierarchy is set – the three, highlighted, forms of decay are the most important points and the ones that will lead the brain on to the rest of the information.

Remember, if Figure 5.1 doesn't look like something that will work for you, don't worry. You can do anything you want. This is only an example of what a spider diagram *might* look like. And it's a very simple one at that.

Actually building a set of spider diagrams in this way is good revision in itself as it forces you to think about how all the information fits together, refreshing your memory and possibly improving your understanding. Once you have them they become an invaluable revision tool, allowing you to review your topics rapidly. Try replicating your diagrams from memory; if they are not the same note where you went wrong and try again. Once you can do this without mistakes you can be sure that you know the topic pretty well.

Mind Maps®

(Mind Map is a Registered Trade Mark of the Buzan Organisation, used with enthusiastic permission.)

Originally developed in the 1960s, Mind Maps® are the concept of celebrated author and brain expert Tony Buzan. A special form of spider diagram, Mind Maps® make use of emphasis, colour, keywords, pictures, association and the principles of recall learning to create as close to a representation of your mind on the page as possible.

Not only do Mind Maps® help you memorise information, they can also help to unlock pockets of understanding that you were previously unaware of. By introducing you to new creative pathways and techniques, Mind Maps® arouse dormant parts of your brain and have the potential to improve your memory and understanding immeasurably.

The process of mind mapping is similar to that of spider diagrams. There are, however, a number of differences:

● Always start in the middle of the page by drawing a large picture that represents the topic you are mapping. Don't worry if you think you can't draw – it doesn't matter.

- The connecting branches that lead away from the middle should start thick and organic (wavy) and become thinner as you move down the hierarchy to the less important key words.
- Single words should be on single lines of the same length.
- Make particular use of colour as this is another good way of linking particular bits of information.
- Make it as attractive to the eye as possible.

You can find more detailed guidance on how to Mind Map® on Tony Buzan's website, www.buzancentres.com. It also features the story behind the original development of Mind Maps® as well as further interesting information and resources.

We have included an example of a Mind Map® that we constructed in Figure 5.2. It covers the broader topic of GCSE-level radioactivity in general rather than focusing on one specific part as in Figure 5.1.

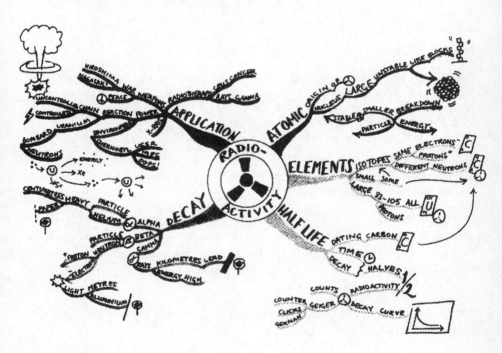

Figure 5.2 Example of a Mind Map®

As with spider diagrams, and memory aids in general, it's best to develop your own style of mind mapping. Stick to the basic principles outlined here and on www.buzancentres.com – these have been specifically designed to make the brain work in a certain way – but incorporate your own creativity and way of thinking. Only then will it be a map of your mind.

Once you have put together a set of Mind Maps® reproduce them on a separate sheet of paper from memory, just as with spider diagrams. If something is different make a mental note then try again. Eventually you'll be able to do it perfectly, which means that if necessary you can do so in the exam – almost like taking your notes in with you!

Bear in mind, however, that mind mapping and indeed spider diagrams can take some time, particularly if you are not used to them. This may be time that you don't have.

The last minute

In fact, if you don't have long left then the memory aids mentioned in this chapter are going to be difficult to include in your revision. Memory aids are supposed to *help* you. If they turn out to be just another thing you are struggling to do they are a waste of valuable time and energy. Thus, in one sense, you would be advised to utilise these techniques only if you have the time to do so properly – otherwise you risk turning up to the exam with nothing to show for yourself but a collection of half-finished pretty pictures.

Having said this, last-minute, emergency revision is all about 'cutting corners' and increasing the efficiency of your limited revision – working smarter, not harder. In such a context memory aids and techniques can play a significant role as they can increase the speed at which you learn. So, if you can develop a way of mind mapping, or producing spider diagrams, or revision cards, or mnemonics, whereby the benefit of doing so outweighs the cost to your time, then by all means do so.

In fact, that goes for everyone revising for exams, not just the last-minute desperadoes. It's almost the examinees' mantra: *If you find something that works for you, use it!*

N is for ...

Next Don't get bogged down. If a question is proving difficult, move on and return to it later.

Notes Should be quick and easy to read whilst covering all the necessary information.

O is for ...

Outline Summarise the main features, emphasising structure rather than detail.

Options You often have a choice of subjects/topics to study. Tailor these choices to areas that interest you, those you are good at and those assessed in ways that benefit you (i.e. coursework vs exams).

P is for ...

Panic Don't do it – it is simply not worth it and will only confuse you. Try to think rationally and maintain calm at all times.

Past papers Invaluable sources of exam information – make use of them.

Planning The key to passing with flying colours.

Post mortem Don't undermine your – and others' – confidence by going over an exam with your friends as soon as it's over.

Procrastination or **Putting things off** The enemy within. Remember, things tend to take twice as long as the procrastinator expects – so start now, not later.

Prove Use evidence or calculations to show why something is so.

Q is for ...

Qualitative Explanations, not calculations.

Quantitative Include numbers and/or equations in your answer.

Quitting There's no point in giving up. Keep trying until the bitter end – it could pay off.

Question Make sure you answer it! Don't waste time listing irrelevant information.

Chapter 6
All gain, no pain

Managing exam-related stress

The single, greatest enemy of the humble examinee is not the examiner; it's not their teachers; it's not even the dark lord Sauron! It's the stress. But then you don't need us to tell you that.

Not content with coupling the pressure of expectation with limitless revision and limited time, the exam gods also saw fit to schedule their little tests slap bang in the middle of summer. Oh, the irony! With the possible exception of Christmas, exam season is the very time of year when potential distractions are at their most prevalent – just when you need them least. This does nothing to help your probably already fragile mental state. In particular, the smell of freshly cut grass wafting in through your open window messes with your head like no other substance on Earth!

In light of these factors stress of some degree is inevitable. It is almost impossible to be so far removed that you don't feel even the slightest pang of anxiety over the impending revision, exams, results, etc. In fact the only students who are likely to achieve such a state of mind are those who really don't care how well/poorly they do and emotionless robots. It's probably safe to assume that neither of these groups will be reading this book so we shall continue under the assumption that they don't exist.

Stress is the result of your body and mind getting together and letting you know that something's wrong. A little stress is a good thing as it tells you that if you want to stay healthy you need to change something about your behaviour. What is not good is if it goes too far and the symptoms of stress (lack of sleep, anxiety, headaches, etc.) start to consume you. When this happens you are in no fit state to prepare for, or take, exams effectively. Your body and mind will spend far too much time on the stress itself to give your work the attention it requires – the greater and more out of control the stress levels the more difficult it is to progress along the Exam Survival Wedge (see page 4) and the more difficult it is to pass exams.

It is vital therefore that you keep the evil stress monster under some degree of control. This usually means taking preventive measures but it could also mean reacting to unforeseen stressful situations. Either way you should have a plan or mechanism in place to deal with the increased stress you are at risk of during the months leading up to your exams. That way your path to survival and success will be as smooth and trouble free as possible.

Objectives and perspectives (2)

Remember how in Chapter 2 we discussed how important it is to have a plan? We talked in terms of doing the best you can, given your circumstances. That meant identifying your starting point on the Exam Survival Wedge, where you want to/think you can finish and how you can go about bridging the gap between these two extremes. This process is pretty much the same as answering the question: 'How can I minimise the stress?'

A good plan, complete with well-defined objectives, strategies, tasks and timetables, serves the dual purpose of taking you as far as you can get in your journey whilst making it as simple as possible to get there. If your plan is good, and it runs without a hitch, then everything should slot into place for you and you can make your way forward in a Zen-like state of calm. Of course this isn't necessarily a realistic portrayal of the exam experience – it is almost impossible to form a perfect plan that accounts for the many different things that can get in the way or go wrong. It is, however, a goal for you to bear in mind when making your preparations so as to help you get as close to perfection as you possibly can.

This is stress management as a pre-emptive strike: by putting in place a plan designed to minimise stress levels whilst maximising achievement you can avoid much of the stress-bringing scenarios commonly faced by examinees. For example, if you construct a revision timetable that works – i.e. allotting sufficient time for each subject, allowing for unexpected blips, including time for breaks, etc. – and then, more importantly, stick to it, you automatically remove the stress associated with running out of time from the equation. Similarly, if you plan and revise according to your syllabuses, you will avoid that horrible feeling of sitting down to an exam paper and not recognising what any of the questions are on about – surely the ultimate in exam stress.

And, as in Chapter 2, just as important as defining and planning your objectives is keeping a healthy sense of perspective. By holding on to what *really* matters and what the reality of your situation is you make sure that obstacles only receive the respect they deserve, rather than needlessly multiplying their significance by ten and suffering the resultant stress-a-thon.

Try to bear in mind the following:

Failure is not the end of the world

… and it is an option, regardless of what others might say or you might think. If you spend too much time and energy worrying about failure, then you are in fact less likely to succeed. Even if it means missing out on your chosen university, 'failing' a set of exams does not prevent you from leading a successful and happy life. Think about how many other important things there are in your life and how passing your exams compares with them.

Don't be over- or under-ambitious

If you attempt to stretch yourself beyond your capabilities you increase the likelihood of a stress meltdown through falling behind. Likewise, if your revision plan is too easy then the sense that you're not doing enough can result in stress rearing its ugly head once again.

Examiners aren't malevolent beasts intent on seeing you fail!

Hard as it might be to believe, they are in fact on the whole very nice people who want to give you every last mark they possibly can. Thinking about this should give you hope during the dark times as you know that there is at least one other person on your side during the exam.

Exams are not there to catch you out

They are instead your chance to shine! Those nice examiners are not trying to trick you into losing marks, but are giving you every opportunity to gain them. Think of it as starting the exam with 0 per cent and then slowly building up your score with every word that you put down. If you think you start with 100 per cent and lose marks with each word you will lose heart and become stressed so much more easily.

The odds are in your favour

Most students pass exams, and abject failure is actually a very rare occurrence. Take heart in the fact that the A-level pass rate is now running at about 90 per cent, and in the year 2000 only 1 in 100 students actually failed all of their A-level examinations. So, even if you've done only a cursory amount of revision you are still probably more likely to pass than win the lottery (and it'll cost you less too).

Everyone is capable of remembering enough

The capacity of your brain to store information is truly incredible. Think about everything you can recall from your life so far – more raw data than you'll ever need to pass an exam, and that's without even trying! So, even if it sometimes feels as if you can't fit anything else in there, you can. And then some.

By remembering these points, and others like them, you will be armed with a psychological shield which you can use to deflect the vicious attacks of stress that impending exams can bring on. This doesn't mean that you should ignore problems, not care or become so laid back that you're horizontal, rather that you should keep the stress safely at arm's length where it can't get in the way of how you calmly address your various predicaments.

This is a particularly useful skill to have if you are one of the desperadoes from Chapter 1. Being under-prepared with not long to go until the big day is like a laboratory for the breeding of stress cells. And as such, in this scenario, your biggest challenge is to keep the stress down to a more manageable level, leaving the way clear for you to do all you can to edge towards surviving the exam. Even in the bleakest of circumstances this can be done, but not if you allow the stress to win and take control of your actions.

Similarly, even if you are relatively well prepared there will often be instances when stress management techniques are invaluable. For instance, if you have been focusing your revision on one half of your syllabus topics only to find that the exam is almost exclusively on the other half, the risk is that you will fall into a state of panic leading to three hours of a furrowed brow, cold sweats and little else. However, by keeping a sense of perspective and employing some of the techniques suggested below you will clear your head and probably find that you know more than you think. The rest is (almost) easy!

An Examiner Speaks ...

'All examiners either are or have been teachers, so we know what it is like for the students answering the questions. We have been on their side of the equation and understand the pressures and constraints they're under. We also know what is fair to expect – when we set the papers and check them for consistency we don't sit in a circle thinking of new ways of making students' lives a misery! Our thinking is firmly based in the capabilities of those who will be sitting the exam.

'When we get the answer books back we are encouraged to mark them positively. In other words, at all times and wherever possible we are looking to award more marks and not take any away. We start each paper thinking that awarding full marks is a possibility, although this very rarely actually happens!'

Stress-busting for the body and mind

Stress is a product of the body and the mind – as such, effective stress management should address both your mental and *physical* well-being. Just as top athletes need to train themselves psychologically as well as physically if they are to perform on the day, so must examinees ensure that their bodies can cope with the rigours of the exam period. After all, there's little use in knowing all your stuff for the exam if illness or fatigue prevent you from getting to your seat and taking it.

Your best bet to achieve peak exam condition, both physically and mentally, is to incorporate into your preparation the creation of a healthy, stress-free environment for your body *and* mind. Doing this as early as possible will help to minimise the subsequent levels of stress you are likely to suffer.

Step one in doing this is to set your objectives and keep perspective as outlined above. This forms the framework for all that you do during the revision and exam period and is thus central to managing stress.

In addition, you should probably consider the following.

Make your room a positive learning environment

A clean and tidy, well-organised space makes the world of difference to your revision. If you have to waste time searching for relevant notes or pencils, or even your bed, you are (a) not learning and (b) probably stressing.

Be open to help

Although how you perform in the exam is ultimately down to you, this doesn't mean you should block everyone and everything else out. While we'll see below that other people can be a disruptive influence on your preparation, they can also be of help. Keep an open mind and be prepared to let others help you stop wasting time heading down blind alleys. Having said this ...

Do things your own way

Whilst help is a good thing to have, it can also create stress by throwing your preparations into disarray. It needn't. If a certain approach or technique was working for you before, don't bin it simply because someone else thinks there's a better way. Even if their way is better it might do more bad than good to introduce it at a late stage in proceedings. If in doubt, stick to what you know.

Eat a good diet

You don't have to be in marathon-running condition to do well in exams, but an exclusive diet of junk food and caffeine will deaden your senses to the extent that working on your mental conditioning becomes increasingly difficult. Eat as much natural and 'healthy' food as you can – you know the sort of stuff: fruit, vegetables, brown bread, etc. – to give you the energy you need to succeed (hmmm, sounds like a jingle on the radio!).

Have lots of breaks and fun

All work and no play makes Jack a dull boy! It also makes for a burnt-out examinee. If possible, allow your brain the time it needs to accept the information you are cramming in. Scheduling breaks and fun things to do (whatever they may be) will help with this as well as taking your mind off any stressful issues and providing good incentives for completing certain tasks.

Try relaxation techniques

Before you reject this out of hand, relaxation techniques needn't mean transcendental meditation or physically challenging sessions of yoga. Something as simple as closing your eyes and taking a few deep breaths or rolling your shoulders can serve to relieve any built-up tension. Light stretching can also help, as can having a glass of water, a lie down or, if you're lucky enough to have a willing pair of hands, a massage.

Get plenty of exercise and sleep

Exercise and sleep are the ultimate in stress releases. They take your mind off the work, they improve your physical health, they are fun (in as much as sleep can be fun), they are great! Of course, if you are stressed about something it could end up affecting your sleep patterns, in which case you should try to employ some other, more conscious, technique to combat the anxiety so that rest comes more easily.

These are the sorts of things that will get your body and mind running together side by side, like finely tuned machines. In such a state the prospect of being derailed by stress is evermore distant.

L'enfer c'est vous autres (Hell is other people) ...

... so wrote existentialist philosopher Jean-Paul Sartre in his play *No Exit* (1944). Apparently he was commenting on something called 'the social and relative tendencies of mankind' but he might just as well have been referring to the contemporary exam experience! Because when it comes to revising for and taking exams there is nothing more annoying or stressful than the contributions that those around you have to make.

Ultimately your exams are all about *you* – what *you* want, how you work, how you perform. However, we all know that there are a number of people with a vested interest in how you get on, and who thus can't stop themselves from getting involved, inadvertently creating a lot of stress and pressure. You know who they are; we mentioned them way back on page 1.

Your parents

It might not always seem like it but they are actually on your side. Every time they badger you about the amount of work you are doing or the time you're spending with your mates, they are doing so with your best interests in mind. They want to see you get some good exam results under your belt so that your options for the future are kept wide open, which really is an excellent way of setting yourself up for a prosperous and happy future.

The best way to handle such 'interference' is to *demonstrate* to your parents that they have nothing to worry about. Their problem is that they cannot see inside your mind and they don't know whether you are going to be ready or not when the exams come around. If they are not convinced otherwise they may well assume that you need some encouragement, even if you don't.

Try making a bit of a show about the revision that you're doing. Let them see your timetable, tell them if you managed to make a breakthrough in your last session or if you got a good mark in a test. Perhaps you could ask them for some help and advice – it may not improve your understanding but it will definitely set their minds at rest that you are taking your exams seriously.

Of course the easiest thing to do is just to talk to them and reassure them that everything is under control. If they're concerned that you're spending too much time away from your desk, calmly explain to them that it is all part of your carefully considered timetable and that you are still on schedule to do well. However, be careful, this is not the cue for an argument. If ever there is a time you don't want a confrontational atmosphere at home it is now. Your exams should be your focus; all arguments do is create unnecessary stress that detracts from the real task at hand. So, even if you think your parents are being unreasonable, it's perhaps worth biting your tongue and looking to compromise wherever possible. They will feel better for it and you will probably save yourself from a lot more grief in the longer run. And you'll almost certainly have the chance to say 'I told you so' later!

It's a different kettle of fish if your parents really *do* have something to worry about. In this case merely convincing them that they don't may get them off your back for a while, but that only becomes worth it if you then use your freedom to get down to addressing your problems. It's perhaps better to be honest with them. Tell them what you think the problem is and then discuss possible solutions. They may even surprise you by being able to help! Remember, they have your best interests at heart.

Unfortunately some parents can get a bit carried away with this and start expecting and demanding levels of effort and results that are simply beyond you. This often happens if they are keen on you following a specific career path that requires exceptional grades – medicine, dentistry, law, etc. This is the worst kind of parental pressure because it is much harder to deal with than common or garden nagging and consequently results in greater levels of stress.

If you are faced with a situation like this, first try calmly talking to your parents, showing as much maturity as you can. Without confronting or accusing them, let them know that you are doing all you can but you fear that they might be expecting too much of you. They might disagree, but try to stay calm and continue with your theme of working hard and accepting the results. Your goal should be for all parties to agree that you can only do your best. You can't do better than your best, even if you want to, so it really isn't worth worrying about meeting unreasonable expectations. Your parents may well think that your best is better than it really is, but try to carry on with what you are doing regardless. You might end up surprising yourself.

Teachers

Teachers are similar beasts to your parents, only they have the benefit of knowing more about the exams and the work you are doing. They will nag and bug you about doing all the right things and addressing gaps in your knowledge and exam technique. They will lecture you on how to plan an essay or force you into doing endless past paper questions. In short, they will do pretty much exactly the same as we do in this book. So we'll not have a word said against them!

Seriously though, whether they are motivated by professional pride or a genuine concern for your future, as your parents are, they are looking out for you and doing all they can to point you in the right direction. And the best thing for you to do is respond accordingly.

Listen to what they have to say and then digest it, calmly and rationally. Is their advice relevant to you? Does it help? Maybe they're talking absolute rubbish, but then again, maybe not – you won't know unless you give them a chance.

Talk to them. Ask for their help where necessary and tell them if what they're asking you to do doesn't fit in with the approach you're taking. Most teachers – particularly the good ones – are flexible in their teaching methods and will be able to adapt their style to suit individual requirements. They may even be willing to provide you with additional one-to-one tutorial sessions, which can be an immense help.

In general, treat them like you do your parents. Be open and honest and show them where you are doing well and, especially, where you are struggling. They will be happy if they can see that you are putting in the effort and are on your way to doing your best.

Friends

At exam time 'peer pressure' takes on a whole new meaning. Like it or not, you will at some stage find yourself comparing what you are doing and how well it is going with your friends and associates at school. Are they doing better than you? Are they working harder than you? Are you being a geek and working too hard? And so on. This process goes ballistic once the exams start and everyone discusses what they do or don't know just as you are entering the exam room, and then where they went right or wrong once you come out … BIG MISTAKE!

Try to avoid casual conversation with your mates about your revision and exams, particularly as the big day gets closer. The only purpose such discussions will serve is to undermine the confidence you have in yourself that you are doing the right thing. You will panic as you suddenly believe that you have been wasting your time all along and that you really should have been doing it their way. You may then try and change your approach for the last couple of weeks, which will of course be counterproductive as it won't fit in with anything you have done so far.

The truth is that taking exams and revising are individual pursuits, despite the fact that so many people do them at exactly the same time and in exactly the same place. Other students' objectives and plans (if they have them) won't necessarily coincide with yours. In fact it is unlikely that they will cross over at all. They will inevitably be focusing on different topics, practising different techniques, taking different styles of notes, using different kinds of tests, and there are bound to be times when they are going out while you are staying in and vice versa.

Friends can be a good source of support and some people find that working with someone else helps, but in general most students will only find stress by working to someone else's agenda. The best thing to do when you're with your friends is to avoid the subject of exams altogether. The chances are that you will be with them at a time when you're on a break from revision anyway, so the last thing you'll want is to be reminded of how difficult memorising the periodic table is!

And do not, repeat, do *not*, discuss the exam with your friends on the day. We cannot emphasise this strongly enough. Months of preparing for questions on x and y can be blown out of the water by your friend innocently uttering the words 'I hope there's something on z' seconds before you sit down to the paper. Your mind will instantly start thinking about how you should have revised z because there'll be nothing on x and y, and the fear will start to set in. Of course just looking at the exam paper should dispel such negative thoughts, but it's not a nice feeling and certainly not the best way to start an exam.

Similarly, once you have been asked to stop writing and you leave the exam room, the words 'Did you put this for question 12?' are sure to reach your ears. That'll be a first-class ticket to Stressville! What if you didn't put that for question 12? Does that mean you got the question wrong? Does that mean you got all the questions wrong? What if you didn't even answer question 12? Should you have done? It all seems so obvious now. 'And what about question 2? That was difficult, wasn't it?' Er, no actually, I thought it was quite straightforward. 'Don't tell me I didn't understand it properly or missed something important ...' and so on.

This is just the kind of post-mortem discussion that can really screw your head up, making you believe that you've failed and there's no point in going on. Relax. The time for reflection is not now. What's done is done and for all you know you did brilliantly. Don't encourage your friends by joining in their conversation; try to block them out and focus on the relief that there's one exam you'll never have to take again.

Everyone else

Everyone, from members of your extended family to strangers in the street, has an opinion. And whether that means expectations are rising or perceived standards are falling, it's an additional headache you could do without. Fortunately, when you don't come into contact with these people every day it's relatively easy just to ignore them and get on with it.

Having said that, specialist TV and radio programmes, books and websites can be a great help and should be sufficiently removed from your everyday life not to stress you out too much. However, be careful; by turning to one of these sources for help and advice you run the risk of creating a 'friend' situation, which can result in your confidence being severely damaged. For example, it is extremely disheartening if a book (any book, even this one) suggests that unless you do it their way you will fail. The thing to do here is prove them wrong – stick with what works for you and pass with flying colours. By all means take on board what they have to say but make sure you then apply it to your own situation.

Remember, it's never too late and you're never a lost cause. Like stress, help can come from anywhere. Keep moving forward and use everything and every person that you can to help make you stronger.

The heat around the corner

Unsurprisingly, stress levels tend to reach their peak in the immediate run up to the exams themselves. Ideally you will be so well prepared and confident at this stage that nothing will worry you (that's the whole point of putting in the work), but it's difficult not to feel at least a bit apprehensive. That's okay. Use it to your advantage, to spur you on, to motivate you; but, as before, don't let it consume you – keep that sense of perspective.

If you are nowhere near ready and you can feel the heat of the exams just around the corner then you can be forgiven for panicking. But stop! And think! Go back and look at Chapter 2. Think rationally about your situation and the objectives you can still set yourself. If it's too late to achieve your initial goals then get some new ones and calmly plan how you can achieve them with the limited time and resources you have at your disposal. Then get stuck in – and try to keep the inevitable stress under control by keeping in mind much of what we have discussed in this chapter and what we will go on to discuss in the next ...

R is for ...

Reconcile Point out how two apparently contradictory points of view can both be true.

Relate Highlight how things are connected. Occasionally it means to narrate (e.g. a story).

Review Make a critical examination or survey.

Revision Learning, understanding, remembering, testing, reflecting.

S is for ...

Short answers Don't let them turn into long answers.

Spider diagrams Method of note taking and revising designed to help recollection and understanding.

State Give a brief, clear presentation.

Summarise Give an account, highlighting key points rather than detailed examples.

Syllabus A very useful tool, whether you start revising two years or two weeks before the exam. It is what the exam and marking scheme is based on and will help you fill in anything you've missed during lessons.

T is for ...

Time There's never enough of it – whether you're revising or in the exam, make the most of what you've got by planning and prioritising.

Timed exam practice The closest thing you'll get to the real thing, without actually being there.

Trace From a certain point, show the history or development of a particular topic.

Chapter 7
The final countdown

Last-minute revision (and nerves)

Ideally you will reach the peak of your powers just as the exams begin. Not too early (so that you lose interest and your brain starts stagnating) and certainly not too late. This is what all the planning and preparation has been about, timing your efforts so that you reach optimal capacity at exactly the right point.

If this is you, then excellent – well done. You don't need to concern yourself that much with actual revision now as it's virtually all been done. Your thoughts can start to turn instead towards the finer points of the exam itself.

Last-minute logistics

It is helpful to sort out in your head what you have to do for the exam well before you get there. This calms any nerves you might be suffering from by removing any potential banana skins of uncertainty – it would be a shame at this late stage to fall foul of schoolboy errors such as turning up in the wrong place or at the wrong time.

You can use past papers to familiarise yourself with the specific instructions for completing each exam. Make sure that you know:

- which papers you are sitting
- on what dates you're sitting them
- where they are and at what time
- how long they last
- the types of questions you will be asked
- the number of questions you will need to answer.

THE FINAL COUNTDOWN

To help you in this you could try producing an 'exam management sheet' for each paper, with all the appropriate information on it. It's up to you how you go about it but it might look something like Figure 7.1.

Subject: *Physics*	
Date: *Wednesday 3rd June*	**Time:** *9.30 (be there at 9.00)*
Building: *Science block*	**Room:** *G12*
Paper: *Paper 4*	**Number of questions to answer:** *Section 1: 6 or 7 compulsory questions* *Section 2: option topics – choose 1 out of 3*

Question No:	Time Allowed:	Marks available:
Section 1 *Section 2*	(Total time: 1 hr 20 minutes) *50 minutes* *30 minutes*	*40 marks* *20 marks*

Checklist:	Notes:
● *Pens and pencils* ● *Rubber* ● *Ruler* ● *Exam entry slip* ● *Pencil case* ● *Mathematical instruments* ● *Calculator and batteries* ● *Spare calculator* ● *Revision notes* ● *Watch* ● *Sweets or drinks*	*Remember to read the Solid Materials and Earth and Atmosphere questions in Section 2 to decide which one to choose.* *Do Section 2 before Section 1 to avoid running out of time.* *Leave Electromagnetic induction question in section 1 until last because it is the hardest topic*

Figure 7.1 Example of an exam management sheet

Sort out how long you need to allow for each question in advance so that you don't end up wasting precious time in the exam. It will be difficult to stick to exactly the planned amount of time for each question on the day, so think about which ones you would be better off spending relatively more or less time on if push comes to shove.

You should also consider the order in which to answer the questions. Obviously you won't know exactly what you are going to be asked, but by examining past papers you can get a pretty good idea of what to expect and where your strengths and weaknesses will lie. Plan to do the 'easy' questions that you are more confident about answering first, leaving the dodgier ones till last when running out of time won't be such a disaster.

Stock up with plenty of stationery and other such equipment. These kinds of things have a habit of going missing just when you need them most, so having a back-up supply is advisable.

Make sure you know exactly where each exam room is, how you get there and how long it takes to do so. It is a peculiarity of taking exams that you will often find yourself in a room you have never been in before, or perhaps didn't even know existed, despite it being in your school, college or university. Don't allow yourself to be surprised by such things on the actual day.

Once you know all of this stuff you are truly ready and everything should click into place quite nicely, thank you very much. The exam itself (see Chapter 8) can become your focus. However, it's possible (maybe even probable) that you won't actually be in such a good position – there is a chance that you will be distinctly under-prepared with not very much time to go.

Desperado times call for desperado measures

Way back in the introductory chapter to this book we promised that we would not ignore the many people for whom best revision practice is not possible. And we haven't, having regularly mentioned how our discussions relate to those of you who are, shall we say, pressed for time. It's a good thing too because the truth is that with only days to go before the action starts many people simply aren't as ready as they would like to be.

But what can they do about it?

Well, first things first: to leave everything until the last minute is quite blatantly not the right way to go about achieving success in your exams. We wouldn't have just spent the last umpteen pages advocating thorough preparation if it was. Therefore, if at all possible, you should choose the route of best practice. However, we also know that this is not always realistic, so we need to consider a slightly different approach, just in case.

Before you start worrying you can rest assured that this doesn't mean rapidly developing a myriad of brand new skills and techniques that we haven't already covered in the previous chapters. You need to instead take all the elements that go to making up 'best practice' exam preparation and apply them to your own situation as best you can.

Objectives and perspectives (3)

As always, the first and most important thing for you to do is define your situation and the task that lies ahead of you. This is as true if you only have two days left as if you have two long years. In fact it is particularly important if you are running out of time because it is essential that you accept the predicament that you're in. There's no point living in denial, swimming against the tide – you've got to acknowledge that you're in a tight spot and need to do something about it, and fast. Even if you would ordinarily be capable of scoring 100 per cent every time you've got to get used to the fact that this time you probably won't.

You should therefore perhaps set your sights a little lower than you'd like. Your plan must be achievable or else you're going to find yourself sitting an exam from the end of a half-finished bridge to nowhere. If you had a good plan that you just didn't stick to you can't cling on to those original objectives and still expect to hit them; you're going to have to reconsider.

You will find that this exercise removes a lot of the pressure and stress that you are no doubt under. As soon as you realise that your goals are achievable you will find it so much easier to motivate yourself to reaching them.

This doesn't mean you should make your objectives easy. You should always look to push yourself as far along the Exam Survival Wedge (see page 4) as you can go in the time you've got left and with the tools at your disposal. Always aim to come out feeling as if you have accomplished something. Besides, if you're starting *really* late, then it's likely that no objective is going to be easy.

In identifying your targets you need to decide whether you'd prefer to know a broad rage of topics a little bit, or fewer topics reasonably well. Both cases represent similar locations on the wedge, which is probably about as far as you can expect to go – you certainly won't have time to get to know a lot of topics really well.

Your decision in this respect will depend on how you see the exam turning out. We have already established that looking through past exam papers is an integral part of any exam preparation, but when your time is limited it helps if you can elevate question-spotting to an art form.

You can often be about 80 per cent sure that a certain selection of questions will crop up in the exam. It's a risky business, but if you can identify these questions, and then focus exclusively on the areas they cover, you will save a lot of time whilst still giving yourself a chance of doing well. There's a large element of luck involved of course, and you will be left hoping for the best somewhat, but it's a strategy that has worked for people in the past and could do for you.

If, however, the paper you're planning for tends to exhibit more variation in the questions it asks and the topics it covers then you'll have to consider spreading yourself a little bit more thinly. This is just as risky as focusing on a narrow range of areas because it will mean you take the chance that your knowledge will be too sketchy to answer certain questions properly. It's not difficult to see that by far the best thing to do is to put months of work in and avoid this situation entirely.

Once you have considered these factors and decided on your objectives – the destination for your (admittedly short) journey – you need to plan how you're going to get there. In other words, your last-minute revision.

Cramming

If anyone ever says to you that if you don't know your stuff the night before the exam you never will, they're talking rubbish. Don't they realise that you have the whole night in which to learn it?! Although it's not a nice situation to be in, if necessary you can use those last precious hours to cram as much information into your short-term memory as you possibly can. It may not stay there for much more than 24 hours, and you probably won't be in peak physical condition come daybreak, but a single equation, word, theory or process that you learned at 2 o'clock in the morning of the exam could very well mean the difference between passing and failing.

Similarly, if you have a few days or weeks left into which to fit months' worth of work, you're going to have to cram as much into the hours you've got left as your sanity will allow. Of course this approach is wholly undesirable and should be resisted with every fibre of your being, but if you have no choice you have no choice. In this case it's always better to keep fighting than to surrender.

Once you've set your objectives (and been quick about it!) you then have to throw much of what we have discussed in the preceding chapters out of the window. You simply won't have time to take lots of regenerative breaks and exercise; good nights' sleep will be harder to come by; making an excellent set of revision notes will be more difficult to manage; and your desk will probably get very messy very quickly.

However, you still need to have a plan and some sort of a timetable to work to. The difference is that you need to be a little bit cannier in your approach. You need to work smarter as well as harder, cutting a few corners and trying to increase the efficiency of the revision you do have time for.

Perhaps you can save time by reducing the number of reviews you do of each area, or by confining the testing stage to a couple of mock questions in your head. You can maybe focus on memorising facts rather than spending time working on your understanding, or concentrate on formulating answers for questions rather than practising your essay-writing skills.

There are many things like this that you can do to edge yourself ever closer to exam survival. You can probably think of many more that would work for you but that we haven't suggested here. Don't be afraid to improvise and try new things but, if they're not working, move on quickly.

Above all, however, be careful. Leaving it all to last-minute cramming is a high-risk strategy – avoid it if you can. It is highly likely that it won't pay off and it can lead you to a lot of stress. And whilst your body can probably cope with a week or two of intensive study – indeed you will probably instinctively be able to work harder during this period than at any other time in your life – any longer than this and your health really will start collapsing in on you.

Stress and the last minute

The last-minute approach makes most of the anti-stress advice of Chapter 6 redundant – there simply isn't the time or opportunity for most of it. This is a shame because it's probably the most stressful experience of the lot. For a short time you will be swamped by your work and the stress that comes with it – but don't despair because there are still ways to keep the beast at bay.

You won't be able to take breaks and exercise as frequently as you would like, but by keeping a sense of perspective, thinking positively (remind yourself what you are doing and why), looking ahead, focusing on achievable tasks, breathing, stretching, etc., you will find it a little easier to complete the task in hand.

Even if you are not a last-minuter and have been preparing for months, it is quite natural for the stress levels to build as the exams get nearer. In this case it should be easier to take time out and relax. Try interrupting every moment of anxiety by thinking (or saying) something like 'I am ready'. It could almost become your mantra. Repeat it enough times and you'll eventually convince your subconscious of what you are already consciously aware of: you are indeed ready.

U is for ...

Under pressure A little pressure is a good motivator but don't let it engulf you – it's not worth it. In particular, try not to let your parents add to your stress levels.

Understanding A much more effective base from which to tackle exam questions than rote learning.

V is for ...

Verify Show why something is true, using evidence.

W is for ...

What ... When ... Where ... Why ...? These questions are often asked. Make sure you answer *exactly* what you're supposed to.

Chapter 8
The moment of truth

Surviving the exam itself

This is it – the exam!

On the face of it exams are just a couple of mornings and afternoons sitting in a quiet but crowded room under the glare of some stern-faced invigilators. An intimate moment between you and your question paper. But of course appearances are deceptive and exams are a lot more than that.

They are what it's all been about, what all your hard work and commitment have been leading to. They are the last piece in a jigsaw that has probably taken the best part of two years to complete. And when they're over, and all the results are in, they will be how your time in academia is remembered. All those years for a couple of grades. So, no pressure there!

Don't worry. The exams themselves may be daunting prospects, and there may be a lot riding on them, but if you have put the requisite amount of effort into your preparation you are sure to find them relatively straightforward.

Imagine a marathon runner who spends a whole year running mile after mile every week in training for their next race. By the time the big day comes around he or she knows that their ability to run can't get much better than it is. They're basically ready to undertake the reasonably simple task of putting in that little extra effort to go a few more miles. If they hadn't put in all that training then the shock to their system of a marathon would probably do them a lot of damage, but as it is they'll be okay.

That is how you should think of your exams – the opportunity to do exactly what you have been doing for weeks, months and years, only that little bit more. And it's easier to raise your game to the next level than you might think – the combination of real exam conditions and the rush of adrenaline that usually kicks in provides you with previously untapped levels of concentration.

But we believe in safety first and leaving nothing to chance. So it is important to make sure that you are fully prepared in every way for every exam, including how to go about answering the questions in such a way as to make the most of your levels of knowledge and understanding. Put another way, what can you do in the exam that will enhance your final position on the Exam Survival Wedge and add that little extra to the end result? Or, what's the quickest route around the marathon course?

The night before

Read your notes

Go through the revision notes and cards that relate to the exam(s) the next day. This serves to refresh your memory of the important material. At this extremely late stage you should ideally only need your notes to jog your memory and shouldn't be trying to learn things for the first time.

However, as we saw in the last chapter, it is possible that even with only a few hours to go you will have significant gaps in your subject knowledge. In these pretty desperate situations you have little choice but to cram in all you can in the time you've got left. But remember, work smart – don't waste any time on anything that isn't absolutely necessary.

Be prepared

Pre-empt the pressure that comes with the morning of the exam by preparing as much as you can the night before. Pack your bag and make sure that you have everything you need (check this against your exam management sheet (see page 85) if you have one, or the checklist below). If you are missing something then better to spend time looking for it now than risk being late to the exam tomorrow. Get your clothes ready too so that in the morning you need only get up, get ready, and go. Don't worry too much about what you're going to wear – it's an exam, not a party, and no one will be paying attention anyway.

Double-check where the exam venue is (again, you can use your exam management sheet) and make sure that you have set your alarm for the right time. You might want to set a second alarm or ask someone to wake you at a given time just to make sure that even if one system fails you won't oversleep. Being well prepared the night before will help give you peace of mind, enabling you to relax and get the good night's sleep you need.

For all your exams you will need:

- pens and pencils – remember to take spares
- an eraser (most exam boards *do not allow* correction fluids such as Tipp-Ex)
- a ruler
- your exam entry slip, which has your candidate number and centre number on it
- a pencil case (remember that you can only have a transparent pencil case or bag on your desk in the exam)
- a watch
- sweets or drinks (if your school or college allows you to have these).

Depending on the subject, you may also need to take:

- mathematical instruments such as a protractor and compasses
- a calculator, plus a spare one or a spare set of batteries
- a dictionary
- a copy of an approved text (annotated if appropriate)
- a cassette walkman.

Stay healthy

We have said before that good exam preparation means keeping your body as well as your mind in good shape. This is particularly true once the exams proper begin. You need to keep your strength up at this time because exams are intense experiences that will drain you both physically and emotionally.

Some students find that pre-exam nerves make them lose their appetite. Even if this happens to you the night before an exam, try and make sure that you eat sensibly. If you can possibly avoid it, don't drink lots of coffee or take caffeine pills to stay awake during the night to revise. Unless it is absolutely (and we mean *absolutely*) necessary, all you are likely to achieve by doing this is make yourself too tired to sit the exam. If you are properly prepared there really is no need for such cramming. Go to bed early and set the alarm to give yourself plenty of time to get to the exam venue instead.

Work by yourself

Even if you have been successfully studying with a friend or group of friends throughout your preparation, now is the time when you're definitely better off staying by yourself. Although other people may be studying for exactly the same exam they will no doubt have different revision needs to you. For example, you can't afford to spend half an hour going over a topic with them that you understand perfectly well. Besides, you need to start getting used to being alone with your thoughts, just as you will be in the exam.

Your friends will also have ways of coping with last-minute nerves that won't necessarily be compatible with yours. In particular, avoid people who may unsettle you with their constant worrying or excessive confidence. If a friend who hasn't been revising properly starts panicking and wants you to come to the rescue, don't feel obliged to help. If their teacher hasn't been able to get them to do the right things in a year, you are not going to be able to help them in just one night!

The morning of the exam

Have a good breakfast

You need to stock up on energy because exams can be very tiring. Eat carbohydrates rather then sugary foods, but don't alter your habits too much. Suddenly feasting on a hundredweight of muesli when all you're used to is a slice of toast is the sort of thing that will play havoc with your insides – the last thing you want to be thinking about in the exam is the noises your stomach is making.

Bananas are an excellent source of energy, and not that filling either, and water is an elixir for the soul (don't drink too much though or you'll be up and down to the toilet all the way through the exam). If you feel a little depleted during the exam itself, a boiled sweet or two can give you the energy you need to help you concentrate. Don't crunch them too loudly though!

Travelling to the exam

Make sure you allow yourself plenty of time to get to wherever the exam is. It may be that it's usually only a ten-minute bus ride but you just know that this will be the day that it's late or held up, or it breaks down or gets lost, so leave a lot earlier than you would ordinarily. And aim to get there with plenty of time to spare. Not only will this negate any delays you might experience but it will also give you the opportunity to settle down and get yourself into the right frame of mind.

Outside the exam

Just like the night before, avoid contact with the panickers and the show-offs as they could unsettle you. This could be difficult if they are your best friends and determined to talk to you. If you have to make conversation keep it low key and stay off the subject of the exam if possible. The best thing to do, however, is to avoid socialising and quietly wish your friends luck just as you go in.

You might like to find a quiet spot where you can read through your revision cards away from the influence of others. By no means should you try and learn something new though – it really is too late now. The main thing to do is get into a calm, relaxed, but focused, state of mind in preparation for the job ahead.

Before you start

Switch off your mobile phone

You're probably not allowed to take your mobile into the exam with you, but if it's in your bag, either under your desk or at the side of the room, it must be off. Repetitive ring tones are a distraction to the other candidates – you can even be disqualified if your phone proves a nuisance. The embarrassment of your phone going off can also be unsettling for you too – there's nothing worse than a hall of people looking at you if you're already nervous. And whatever you do, don't answer it, not even if it's a text message – not unless you want to be accused of cheating.

Find your seat

When you go into the exam room don't plonk yourself down any old where. Your desk should already have your candidate details on it – this is where you are to sit. If you can't find where you should be sitting then ask one of the invigilators as soon as possible. In the unlikely event that you have made a mistake and gone to the wrong venue, asking about it early may help you to get to where you should be on time.

Fill in your candidate details

When asked to do so you will have to write some personal details on the front of your answer booklet. These include:

- your name
- your school centre number
- your candidate number
- the paper you are sitting.

Make sure you do this clearly and accurately so as to avoid confusion for the examiners and administrative staff later. If it's not clear who sat the exam, or where, or which exam it was, then there's a risk that your results will be delayed, or even lost altogether.

Check the exam paper

Check that you have the right paper and that it is the one you expected. If it appears wrong then tell an invigilator as soon as possible so you can clear up any mix-ups without wasting any more time.

It's important to read the exam paper rubric (rules) to remind you of how many questions, and which questions, you need to answer. You should do this even if you are sure that you already know what you need to do. There have been lots of cases where even the best students have made silly mistakes under exam day pressure that ended up costing them precious marks.

Lastly, don't open the paper until instructed to do so.

Managing the exam

Choosing questions

You don't have to start writing straight away. Take a little time to read the paper through and double-check the instructions. This will help you to relax, assess the state of play and choose which questions you should do first.

Consider the following:

- What precisely is each question asking you to do?
- Which part of your syllabus does it refer to?

As you go through the paper, circle the questions that you think you can do. Highlight the ones you feel particularly happy about. If two questions seem similar, double-check for any ways in which they are different. You don't want simply to regurgitate an answer if it doesn't address the question completely.

Whether you have a choice of which questions you answer or not, start with the ones that you are most confident about. That way you will build up your score more quickly and efficiently. If you spend a lot of time early in the exam on the questions you're not so sure about you will only manage to pick up relatively few marks, whilst risking having less time to shine with your best topics later.

Make sure that, when you are reading through the paper, you turn over *all* the pages, including the back one. You would be surprised at the number of examinees who miss out on easy questions simply by not looking at the back page. Indeed this particular author once thought he was very clever to finish an exam half an hour before everyone else, only to be told later on that he had neglected to answer a quarter of the questions!

An Examiner Speaks ...

'Definitely, certainly, absolutely the most important thing for a candidate to do is answer the question! I used to say this when I was a teacher and, if anything, I'm more of an advocate now. Our mark schemes are based around the question, so if the answer isn't there it's not easy to award the marks, to say the least. It is frustrating to see that a candidate has wasted an awful lot of time writing an awful lot of words for absolutely nothing.'

Dissecting a question

Once you're reasonably sure of the precise task ahead of you, you should work out more precisely what each question is asking you to do. Read and re-read the question, highlighting any key words or instructions. It may be that the question is different from what you first thought and you need to consider choosing another.

Immediately note down any relevant and important ideas, phrases or points that come to you. This will help you to formulate your answer when you come back to that question later, and perhaps even remind you why you chose it in the first place.

If you find that you cannot do a question then don't spend too long on it. Always try to come up with an answer, but don't waste time trying to force the issue – you can always return to it at the end if you have time.

Timing

In exams, as in life, good timing can be everything. A good way of organising yourself is to allocate the amount of time that you spend on each question according to the number of marks available. So, if one question is worth half the marks available in the exam, spend roughly half the time answering it. Make a quick note of the time you have for each question and put your watch on the table.

You can be flexible and not stick to your time allocations rigidly – perhaps you don't need as long as you've allowed to put together a good answer, or maybe you need a little longer – but, whatever you do, don't fall too far behind schedule. If this starts to happen move on, because you can't afford not to attempt every question. You can always go back later.

The importance of answering all the questions required of you cannot be stressed enough. If you leave any out you will not be awarded any marks for them, which can seriously affect your result. Whilst you should definitely start with the 'easiest' questions and get some marks under your belt, some students make the mistake of spending too much time on questions that they are more confident about, barely attempting those that they are not. This is usually a bad strategy, for a number of reasons:

- There are only so many marks awarded for each question – you may already have got them all, in which case spending another half an hour answering it will be a waste.
- Simply adding more bulk to an answer doesn't necessarily make it better or more comprehensive – i.e. you've already got all the marks you're ever going to get, so move on.
- If you approach the question correctly you should be able to finish it in the allocated time – if you carry on much beyond this there is possibly something wrong with your answer.
- The less time you leave for other questions the fewer marks you are likely to get – even if you can't complete the other answers you will still be able to pick up some credit here and there.
- The less time you leave for the more difficult questions the less likely you are to answer them – given a bit of time you might be able to work them out, winning plenty of marks in the process.

The key is to strike a balance between the relative difficulty of each question, the time you have left, the marks available and the marks you think you can get. It's a largely improvisational process and you may have to trade off one thing for another, but if you keep the aim of scoring as many marks as possible at the forefront of your mind it should all fit into place.

Handwriting and corrections to your work

First of all you can relax, because you don't need to write as neatly in the exam as you do for everyday schoolwork. The examiners know that exam conditions mean that you are working quickly and under pressure and won't dock marks if your handwriting isn't immaculate. Having said that, if they can't read what you have written they won't be able to award you the marks you deserve, so be careful.

If you make a mistake you only need cross it out with one, clear line. The instructions from the exam boards ask you to do this. Don't try to block words out completely, or scribble all over your work, as this will make your script untidy. Remember that you aren't allowed to use correction fluid such as Tipp-Ex – doing so takes too long anyway.

An Examiner Speaks ...

'As an examiner you have no choice but to be a bit of a code breaker. To be able to decipher handwriting is a valuable skill because it is rare to have a set of answers that are written up in exquisite script. However sometimes, no matter how good our skills, we simply cannot read what has been written, which makes it impossible to award the marks.

'Accurate spelling is another consideration for us. Sometimes, usually in language papers, it is an important part of the mark scheme – in which case not only do candidates have to get the correct spelling but they also have to write it legibly enough for us to see that they've got the correct spelling.'

Short-answer and multiple-choice questions

Many exams do not require you to answer essay questions. Mathematical and scientific subjects, for instance, do not lend themselves well to assessment by essay. And GCSE-level exams rarely require your answers to be long discussions, as their emphasis is on assessing your broad knowledge of the fundamentals rather than your ability to explore a topic to its conclusion.

You will find therefore that you'll probably have to take a number of short answer and/or multiple-choice papers.

At first glance these types of exams may appear to be relatively easy. After all, you're asked a straight question, you give a straight answer and then move on. In the case of multiple choice the answer is even given for you! However, such questions can prove just as difficult to answer as a 45-minute essay. What if you simply don't know the answer? Unlike essay papers you don't often have the choice of whether you answer a particular short or multiple-choice question or not, so you can't leave a difficult one out altogether. Neither can you waffle for a bit and hope to cover up your lack of knowledge – if you don't know, you don't know, and it'll be there for the examiner to see in black and white.

Having said that, there is a knack to taking these kinds of exams, and a few simple things you should bear in mind to make the most of your chance to shine.

Know your stuff

Sounds obvious, but that's because it's so true and so important. Short answer and multiple-choice exams are first and foremost tests of your knowledge. If you don't put in the time and effort to learn facts, methods, vocabulary, theories, etc., you won't be able to draw on them in the exam, which means you won't be able to answer all the questions. Simple as that.

Practice makes perfect

Shorter papers don't usually ask you merely to list some facts or replicate a formula or two; they are far more likely to challenge you to apply your knowledge to the specific context of the question. This is relatively straightforward as the point behind the question – i.e. the piece of knowledge it is testing – is never buried particularly deep. And the best way of learning how to spot what the question is asking you to do is to practice past papers.

There's a limit to the number of ways you can be asked to display knowledge of a certain concept or topic and, if you answer enough past questions, you will probably see them all. Short-answer papers are also relatively quick and easy to do and they are more easily marked, which will give you a good idea of your progress so far and what you still need to work on. So churn out as many as you can and by the time the exam comes around you'll almost be able to do it with your eyes closed!

Look at the question

Just as you need to be aware exactly what an essay question is asking of you in order to answer it properly, you need to pay very close attention to how short questions are presented. In particular, look at:

● the marks available
● the space available.

Consider the GCSE Maths question shown in Example 8.1.

Example 8.1

(b) Solve this equation.

$2x^2 + x - 3 = 0$

....

....

....

Answer x = _____ [3]

First of all you need to ascertain what you are being asked to do – in this case you just need to solve a simple quadratric equation, no application is required.

Now, there are three marks up for grabs and three lines for you to use here – two clues as to what the examiner wants to see in a good answer. Three lines of space must mean that they want to see some working out – i.e. a representation of your thought process and how you arrived at the answer. There is probably one mark allocated for this aspect. If you were to put down only the correct answer, you'd still be awarded full marks, but if your answer were wrong you would get none. By including your working you should earn yourself a mark and a little insurance against getting the wrong answer. That leaves two more marks for you to get, which in this case will be the two possible values for x. That's all you need. No more, no less.

For every question you do (it doesn't have to be a Maths question) look at your answer and check that you can see where the marks will come from. In this example it's one for the working out and one each for the two possible answers. Other questions worth more marks might require a number of steps to get to the final answer; each one of these will be worth something.

Multiple choice

As with short questions, hours of practice make multiple choice so much easier. The way questions are worded in these exams can be deliberately confusing, forcing you to think carefully about what you're being asked. If you already have hundreds of similar questions under your belt then you'll be less troubled by such hurdles in the exam. Unfortunately this doesn't just mean watching endless editions of *Who Wants to be a Millionaire?*, as you will find that examination multiple choice questions take a slightly different approach to Chris Tarrant!

If possible, when you are answering a multiple choice question, try to think of the answer before you read the options. This will make the right answer leap out at you more easily when you do read them and will save you from being misled by something you think might be right, but you're not sure.

If the answer is not obvious in this way you should work through each option given in turn, assessing its validity. Some will be obviously wrong, others less so, leaving you with a reduced multiple choice for you to contemplate – just like taking a 50:50 lifeline. If you're still not sure of the answer, move on and go back to it later. If the worst comes to the worst you can always take an educated (or otherwise) guess, but make sure you leave it until the last possible moment before you choose this particular route.

Whatever you do, you mustn't answer a question without having read all the options. Even if you know the answer off the top of your head and option (a) seems to correspond with it, it may be subtly worded so that it is wrong. If you move on without reading options (b) to (d) you will miss the actual correct answer, even though you knew it.

Finally, pay careful attention to how you are supposed to present your answers. Do you have to circle your choice or write down your answers on a separate sheet? Is there a special answer sheet that will be marked by a computer? Whichever method you need to use, make it crystal clear which option you are going for.

An Examiner Speaks ...

'Short-answer exam papers have very clearly defined mark schemes that we must follow to the letter, which makes them relatively quick and easy to do.

'Essay questions are far more subjective but we do still have a solid framework within which to work. We are provided with detailed descriptions of what constitutes an 'A grade' answer, what's a 'B grade' answer, a 'C' and so on. We then have to decide in our own minds how what we are reading corresponds with the descriptions. We have regular standardisation meetings where we compare notes and make sure that our interpretations of different grades are not too different.'

Essay questions

Essay questions are most prevalent in examinations for Arts, Humanities and Social Science subjects. And they take a little more time than multiple choice!

In some papers, particularly at A2-level, a whole hour might be allocated to a single question. In other exams, and more so at AS-level, you might have as little as 30 minutes. This alarms some students who wonder how on earth they can write a proper essay in that amount of time. There is no need to worry. Remember that everyone is in the same boat and that the examiner *expects* your answer to be shorter and less detailed than an essay for which you have an hour or longer.

As with most things exam-related there is an art to good, timed essay writing. Although you may know your subject well, unless you are able to put your knowledge and understanding on paper in the time allowed you will not be doing yourself justice. And this doesn't mean simply telling the examiner everything you know about a topic either. With the limited time available it is of paramount importance that the information you are able to include in your answer is relevant to the specific question. One of the biggest complaints from examiners is that candidates actually fail to answer what they have been asked. In order to ensure that your answer is relevant you need to prioritise and then include only the key points and facts. To do this you need to plan.

Planning your essay

The order in which ideas and facts are recalled or generated in your mind may make sense to you because they are a result of your own thought process. However, this order is often quite random and may not make any sense to the examiner. You therefore need to organise the information so that your essay reads as a coherent and carefully sequenced response to the question and not a disorganised stream of consciousness.

Plans should be very brief. Remember, you don't have much time and need to get down to writing the actual essay as soon as possible. It will take you too long to write a clear plan that the examiner can follow, so it's best to use a quick note form that you understand. If you do not manage to complete an essay the examiner may refer to your plan to see what you were getting at. However, in that eventuality it is more likely that you will have completed the essay in note form rather than rely on your, possibly incoherent, plan.

Generally it's best to think of clear, separate points that address the question. You might also wish to jot down the examples/evidence that you will use to demonstrate your point.

How long should I spend on planning?

This depends on how long you have to write the essay. When you have a full hour for an essay it is a good idea to spend up to 10 minutes planning. For a shorter essay for which you have 30 minutes, 5 minutes is a sensible time. Some students worry that if they spend this much time on planning they will not have enough time to write the essay. However, planning will actually *save* you time because you won't end up wasting time thinking about what should come next – you will already have your answer mapped out and can simply write it up. Students who don't plan may look as if they are ahead because they started writing first, but they will inevitably have to pause to think later.

Essay structures and argument

Every essay can be divided into three broad sections:

Introduction

- Address the question directly in your first sentence.
- Outline your answer to the question.
- Include any relevant background information.
- Use words from the question.
- Don't discuss examples.

The introduction should be quick and to the point. It may seem as if there's a lot to include, but if you're skilful enough you can cover the above points in two or three sentences. It certainly shouldn't take more than a paragraph.

Argument

- Include a series of key points that address the specific question asked.
- Use paragraphs to separate points/ideas.
- Demonstrate your points using appropriate evidence.
- Use quotes if necessary.

THE MOMENT OF TRUTH

It is extremely important that your argument makes sense! In other words you need to be sure you know what you're talking about. The best way to do this is to plan your answer as above so you don't end up surprising yourself or running down a blind alley. And you should always take the easiest route, sticking to what you know. The exam is not the time to start forming crazy new theories that may or may not work out – it's usually best to stick to accepted thinking which, after all, is what's on the syllabus. By all means include your own personal opinion, just don't let it get in the way of answering the question, and be sure to include some justification for your position.

Conclusion

- Tie together the threads of your argument.
- Summarise what the preceding discussion has shown.
- Answer the question directly.

In answering the question directly you don't have to stick your neck out and subscribe to a particular point of view (unless of course that is what the question asks you to do). Essay questions are usually about *discussing* a particular topic, not *resolving* it.

Don't under any circumstances introduce anything new in your conclusion unless perhaps you have an interesting suggestion for further discussion in light of your answer.

Question types

As with short-answer and multiple-choice questions there are only so many different kinds of essays you can be asked to write. Be aware of how different words ask you to do different things. For example:

- *Compare* – indicate the similarities and differences between.
- *Contrast* – set in opposition in order to bring out differences.
- *Explain* – give a clear account of; give reasons for.
- *Define* – set out the precise meaning of; consider alternative definitions.
- *Illustrate* – make clear using concrete examples.

- *Discuss* – Investigate or examine by argument; give reasons for and against.
- *Account for* – give reasons for.
- *Justify* – show the grounds/evidence for reaching a conclusion; answer the main objections.
- *Outline* – give the main features or general principles, omitting minor details.
- *To what extent* – look at the arguments both for and against a premise.
- *Trace* – show the evolution of.

You will find other examples located in the 'A–Z' boxes at the end of each chapter throughout this book.

Analysis vs description

A good essay is built around analysis of a topic rather than its description. For example, in an English essay there is no need to summarise the plot – you can safely assume that the examiner knows it. Instead you need to present clear points and assertions, based on evidence within the text. This will involve referring to what happens, but only to back up what you are saying.

Summary of essay question dos and don'ts

Do:

- read the question carefully
- plan your answer
- include a clear introduction, argument and conclusion
- use full sentences and paragraphs
- use formal language.

Don't:

- start writing without planning, even if you're running out of time
- begin answering a question before you have read the others
- write in note form (unless you have run out of time)
- write in a block of text without paragraphs
- use abbreviations, unless they are part of accepted subject terminology

- make points or assertions without backing them up with evidence
- indiscriminately write down all you know about the topic
- use slang or colloquialisms.

Having a nightmare

Sometimes, despite all the revision and exam practice, things go a bit wrong and you feel as if you are left sitting in the middle of a nightmare. Perhaps the wrong questions have come up, or you suddenly can't remember a thing, or you've run out of time. What can you do when faced with such a disaster?

First of all, relax; it's only the evil stress monster whispering in your ear and it's not as bad as you think. Then calmly consider what the solution to your problem might be.

Going blank

There aren't many worse feelings than the blind panic which comes with the realisation that you just can't remember. But it needn't last because deep down you know that you know what the answer is and it's just a matter of coaxing it out of your memory.

Start with what you *can* remember and work from there. Go back to the simplest ideas and build on them. Try to relax, as tension may be behind your thought paralysis. Picture where you were when you last revised this topic and note down anything that you can remember – seeing your thoughts on the page will help you regain your focus as well as jog your memory.

Getting the wrong questions

This can be the most disheartening situation of them all – all that time you spent revising *Macbeth* inside out and the Shakespeare question turns out to be on *Hamlet*! Fortunately, for the better-prepared student it's generally not a problem as they will have revised a sufficient number of topics to account for all eventualities, but that's not to say it doesn't happen.

As with going blank, if you are faced with this particular disaster, start with what you *do* know. Even if the topics in question did not form part of your core revision you might have covered them a little bit and you definitely did them in your lessons. So pick out questions that at least ring a bell and see if you can relate them to the themes and theories of which you do have detailed knowledge. Then try and build an answer, little by little, using the limited knowledge at your disposal. This is where good essay writing technique comes into its own because a well-structured and well-written essay that addresses the question can actually disguise the occasional gap in knowledge. It won't see you receive top marks but it will be a lot better than nothing.

Running out of time

Following our advice on managing your time in the exam on pages 99 and 106 should ensure that you don't experience anything more than a slightly mad rush to get a question finished right at the end of proceedings. However, if life were that simple there'd be no such thing as exams in the first place!

If you do find that the clock is beating you, don't panic. If you complete your answers in note form you will still accrue some marks, but if you give up and fail to get down as much relevant information as you can you could lose those vital few marks that will get you a higher grade. If you are struggling with a question early on, leave it and return to it later when you have some good answers under your belt.

An Examiner Speaks ...

'Candidates who run out of time should definitely include any plans or notes they have made during the exam. It is the sensible thing to do because they will pick up credit for the points they include – we know that sometimes it's difficult to complete three or four masterpieces in a couple of hours.

'What we don't like is reading half an essay that just stops without giving us any idea of where it is going. This is not the sensible thing to do because it usually means that the question hasn't been fully addressed and we have no choice but to assume that it hasn't been answered – i.e. no marks.'

After the exam

The best thing you can do in the immediate aftermath of an exam is to forget it ever happened. There is nothing you can do about it once it's done, and spending time obsessing over whether you got this right or that wrong will only cause you unnecessary stress.

To this end, avoid discussing your answers with your friends. This will probably unnerve you. You might end up thinking that you have done badly and this will undermine your confidence for the rest of your exams. Equally, you don't want to upset a friend who has perhaps answered a question incorrectly.

Similarly, leave the question paper in the exam so you aren't tempted to analyse your performance too soon. If you want to keep it for future reference then that's okay, but don't look at it until you have moved on to your next concern, whether it's your next exam or a night out to celebrate.

You may have two exams on the same day. After the morning session it is important to:

● take a break
● have something to eat
● find somewhere peaceful to read through your notes.

The latter point is particularly important when your second exam is in a different subject and you have to switch from intense concentration on one subject to another.

Chapter 9
All about coursework

How to make the best of it

Many subjects at GCSE, AS and A-level involve coursework. Coursework is a general term that covers units (or parts of units) that do not have written examinations done under timed conditions. It can take a number of forms. Some examples are given below:

- A series of scientific experiments or investigations in Biology, Chemistry or Physics.
- Extended research or essays if you study subjects such as Sociology, History of Art, or Modern Languages.
- Creative projects (designing magazine covers or producing a short radio broadcast) in Media Studies.
- Analysing scenes from plays in Drama or Theatre Studies.
- Analysis of a novel or a play if you study English Literature.
- The design of a database in Information Technology.
- Producing a series of sketchbooks in Art.
- Performances in Music or Theatre Studies.
- An analysis of a business idea in Business Studies.
- A study in Geography based on concepts and issues related to the course.
- Studies in History which might be based on a specific country.
- A folio of compositions in Music.
- A collection of photographic work in Photography selected from categories such as Photojournalism, Fashion and Portraiture.
- An experimental investigation in Psychology.
- A series of pieces of creative writing in English Language.

Some subjects can be very heavily weighted towards coursework. The obvious examples of this are Art, Ceramics and Photography. In these subjects, you are assessed on the coursework projects that you undertake throughout the course. Even in the 'examination' components, you might be given the exam question a month or two before the exam period and you use the time for research and preparation.

Coursework is usually marked by your teachers, who then send in a sample to the examination board who will moderate the marks against marks gained by other candidates who are sitting the examinations at other centres.

Advantages of coursework

- Some people find that they do not cope very well with examination pressure. Coursework can relieve this.
- If you are good at planning, organisation and research, then coursework can be a very effective way of gaining lots of marks.
- Often mistakes, omissions and errors in a piece of coursework can be rectified before final submission. If you make a mistake in an exam there is nothing that you can do about it afterwards.
- Coursework allows you to demonstrate the full range of your creativity or knowledge and understanding.
- In many instances, you will be given the freedom to choose what your coursework is about and so you will be able to concentrate your efforts on areas of strength.

Disadvantages of coursework

- Coursework can be very time-consuming.
- If you are not good at organising and structuring your time, or at meeting deadlines, you will find coursework projects very demanding.
- Examiners are aware that coursework is normally less stressful than written examinations and so it can be harder to gain high marks in a coursework unit.
- The rules about getting unfair help are strict and you need to be able to avoid the temptation to get assistance.

Useful points to remember

Check the syllabus

Before you begin a piece of coursework, make sure you know exactly what is expected of you. Remember that coursework requirements differ from subject to subject and from syllabus to syllabus, so consult your teacher if there is anything you are uncertain about. You might even be allowed to see samples of coursework submitted by students in previous years. They are usually returned to schools by the examination boards several months after the relevant examination sitting. This could prove extremely helpful, particularly if you are uncertain as to how your coursework should be planned, structured and presented. You might also find it useful to download the coursework section of the subject syllabus from the Internet (Examination boards' website addresses: www.edexcel.org.uk, www.aqa.org.uk, www.ocr.org.uk, www.wjec.co.uk.). This is certainly one way of ensuring that you know everything there is to know about the examiners' rules and regulations. You should also be able to gain access to detailed mark schemes for coursework. This will help you to keep in mind exactly what you are being tested on and what weighting is given to particular skill areas.

Plan effectively

The structure of your coursework is something that requires a great deal of thought. What is the title of your piece? Are you supposed to include a plan and a bibliography? How long should your coursework be?

Choose your title carefully

If the title of your coursework is left up to you, be sure to come up with something that you know you can explore and develop. The syllabus you are following may well insist that a title has an analytical and evaluative slant as opposed to a merely descriptive one.

ALL ABOUT COURSEWORK

Follow your plan

If you have to include a plan, this is likely to be in bullet-point form. Be sure to keep it clear and concise and remember that each point must be expanded upon within the coursework piece.

Prove your research

The bibliography is your opportunity to show the examiners how carefully and how well you have carried out your research. Whatever materials you have consulted in the preparation phase of your coursework will almost certainly have to be declared. However, remember that you are *not* allowed to reproduce entire chunks of text in your coursework that you have found elsewhere. Nor should you try to pass off somebody else's ideas or words as your own. In short, what you write must be all your own work. The items listed in your bibliography should be sources you have consulted, not copied from.

Keep to the word count

As for the all-important word count, it is unwise to write less than the stipulated minimum or more than the permitted maximum. Do not assume that examiners will not count the number of words you have written. They will, and you will be penalised for not adhering to the guidelines concerning length.

Follow your timetable

Draw up a timetable for your coursework. Take into account your teacher's advice and bear in mind your strengths and weaknesses when it comes to working independently and working to a deadline. Your timetable should consider the following questions:

What is the final deadline for the coursework?

Whatever it is, aim to get your final piece in several days earlier. That way, you can avoid the usual last-minute disaster scenarios ('my computer broke down', 'my printer wouldn't print' and 'I know it's due in today but I wasn't very well last night' are three of the most common!).

When should I begin my research and how long should I allow for this?

Simple. Begin straight away. The more research you do, the more knowledgeable and confident you feel. Allow as much time as possible for your research and avoid the alternative at all costs, which is to start your coursework late, do insufficient research and write an essay that lacks breadth, depth and evidence of independent reading and investigation – all essential skills referred to in coursework mark schemes.

How many drafts will my teacher require me to submit?

At least one. Quite possibly, more. But however many you are allowed, make sure you get them in on time. In other words, treat draft deadlines as you would treat the final coursework deadline. The more efficient you are in the submission of drafts, the more time you will have to make improvements to subsequent drafts and, crucially, to the final coursework piece itself.

And finally

Above all, remember to take your piece of coursework as seriously as you would take a written examination. In other words, prepare for it thoroughly and do all you can to ensure that it is an accurate reflection of your knowledge and ability.

ALL ABOUT COURSEWORK

X is for ...

X At the end of a multiple choice paper, check to make sure that you put the Xs in the right boxes.

Y is for ...

Yesterday When all your troubles seemed so far away! It is important that whilst you don't forget the problems you had yesterday you should keep moving forward. Don't dwell on anything.

You Only you can possibly know whether you're ready for an exam, or how best you should approach it (not your parents, not your friends, not even your teachers, just you). Make sure you do.

Z is for ...

Zenith Ideally, you should be at the peak of your powers just as the exams begin.

The end

If you have just finished your final exam, then our advice is simple. Give yourself a mental pat on the back for having got through them (an achievement in itself), breathe a sigh of relief and then do something really enjoyable to celebrate. And remember, the more exams you pass, the more celebrating you can do - that's what exam survival is all about!